Acclaim for *Falling off Broadway*

"David Black has written a fascinating account of his prestigious career in the theatre. Thoroughly enjoyable."
—Hal Prince

"Winning! Another welcome valentine to the theatre."
— Joel Grey

"Always insightful, always with humor, David Black's Falling off Broadway *is a terrific read."*
— Olympia Dukakis

"David Black has crafted a compelling memoir about Broadway and his years in the trenches producing more than 18 shows."
— Charles Busch

"Falling off Broadway, *David Black's new memoir, is funny and surprising."*
— Alan Arkin

"David Black's Falling off Broadway *is utterly hilarious and irresistible."*
— Louis Begley

Also by David Black

The Actor's Audition

The Magic of Theater

•••••••••••••••••••••••••••••••••••

Falling off Broadway

Published by Mezzo Books

Copyright © 2014 by David Black

ISBN: 978-163192-325-8

Alix,
9 enjoyed our talk..."
Best
David
September 27
_2015_

FALLING OFF
BROADWAY

By
David Black

With thanks to Dr. Fred Kass

For introducing me to myself

TABLE OF CONTENTS

ACKNOWLEDGMENTS

Thanks to the following people for creative ideas and encouragement during the writing of this memoir. They are Beth Walker, Larry Freundlich, Charles Nelson Reilly, David Jepson, Edgar Levenson, Mark Desjardins, Manny Hellman, Elsie Aidinoff, Connie Gore, Liz Rivers, Al and Sandra Hutchinson, Tim and Kate Love, Paul Janssens, Alissa Kaplan Michaels, and Louis Begley.

My wonderful agent, Diane Cleaver, arranged for Vintage Books to publish *The Actor's Audition,* and for LuAnn Walther to be my exceptional editor. Diane also arranged for Macmillan to publish *The Magic of Theater* and found Mark Chimsky to edit it.

Mark Chimsky understands every nook and cranny of the editing business and he brings to it a contagious energy and enthusiasm. I wanted to have the experience of working with Mark again so I invited him to be my editor for *Falling off Broadway,* and I was not disappointed.

Finally, this book would not have happened without my talented wife, Anne Rivers, who contributed ideas and helped edit the manuscript while pursuing her own career. Anne plays a leading role in this memoir, as she continues to do in my life. I am infinitely grateful for her magic, and her love.

The Greatest Show off Earth!

The first show I ever produced was called "The Greatest Show off Earth!" I produced it, wrote it, directed it, and appeared in it at the age of 12, in my grandfather's living room. My grandfather was Emil Goldmark, a lawyer for the *New York Times*. He lived in a large apartment overlooking Central Park West. His maid wore white gloves. Before dinner my grandfather drank sherry and ate watercress sandwiches without the crusts. During dinner, my grandfather told me to look at him. Then he stuck peas up his nose.

After the main course, the maid brought fingerbowls with doilies.

My grandfather picked up his fingerbowl and flicked the doily underneath as far as he could across the table. Then he put his fingerbowl down where the doily had landed. Then it was my turn. I picked up my fingerbowl and tried to flick my doily further than my grandfather's. After dessert, the maid brought a box of chocolates. My grandfather felt each chocolate before selecting one. After the chocolates, the maid brought a box of cigars. My grandfather chose one and clipped it with a gold cigar cutter he kept on a chain. Then my grandfather told me to light his cigar. I lit a match and my grandfather sneezed and the match went out. I lit another match and my grandfather sneezed again and the match went out. When my grandfather's cigar was finally lit, my grandfather told me to put my finger on his nose. When I put my finger on my grandfather's nose, smoke came out of his ears.

On Sunday mornings my mother told me to tiptoe around the house because my father was working on his talk. Then she took me to hear my father speak at the Ethical Culture Society. My father was Algernon Black and my mother was Elinor Goldmark Black. I sat with my mother in a wooden pew upholstered in green velvet. There were stained-glass windows, gothic arches, and ushers with perfumed carnations. While we waited, a powerful organ played. My father sat on a raised platform gazing thoughtfully over the heads of several hundred faithful parishioners. There were flowers at his feet and over his head letters in gold said "The Place Where Men Meet to Seek the Highest Is Holy Ground." When my father got up to speak, the organ stopped.

"Most religions promise hell or heaven if you're bad or good," said my father, "but the truth is there is no afterlife! Man makes his own hell or heaven right here on earth! The most important thing in life is not what you believe, it's what you do because of what you believe. There is no God with a long white beard who will solve the problems of the world!" Then, my father sat down and the organ played loud, joyous music.

There's no God. There's no God! Then what are all these people doing here? I know! They must be here to worship my father! My father is God!

At the end of my father's talk, I stood in a line to shake his hand. When I shook my father's hand he asked me, "Was I any good?"

It seemed to me that my father was in show business. He had a theater with seats to fill and people came to see him perform. On Sunday mornings, before telling his congregation what was wrong with the world, my father sat under a sun lamp to improve his tan.

The most impressive part of my father's performance was the organ. It was so powerful it could only be played by the organist from Radio City Music Hall. The Sunday morning services at the Ethical Culture Society could not begin until the organist had finished playing the early show at Radio City. While I watched from my pew, the ushers with perfumed carnations became archangels endowed with my father's eminence. When the powerful organ shook the rafters, the platform on which my father sat rose higher and higher until he occupied a pedestal reserved only for the God he said did not exist.

My mother worshipped my father, along with everyone else, and it was hard to get her attention. I told jokes and made funny faces. "I may be laughing," said my mother, "but I am not amused."

Whenever I was introduced as my father's son, the reverent greetings convinced me I was also destined for something important. The only problem was I didn't know what it was. Where could I go to study saving the world?

I need something important enough to make my mother tell my father to tiptoe around the house.

One day, when no one was around, I climbed up to the organ loft at the Ethical Culture Society and sat down at the great keyboard. I pulled out the stop that said "Full Orchestra." Then, I stretched my legs till my feet reached the pedals and brought my hands down as hard as I could on the keys. A mighty sound came out of the organ's pipes. I pretended I was the organist at the Sunday service. My mother was watching from her pew. My father was waiting to speak.

He will have to go on waiting until I have finished.

* * *

"Your table manners are so bad," said my mother, "no woman will have you for a husband.

"I don't want to get married."

"If you don't finish all the food on your plate you can't have any dessert!"

"I have two stomachs, one for the main meal and one just for dessert."

"You should be a lawyer," said my mother, "because you have an answer for everything!"

I threw up in front of the Museum of Natural History. Some people laughed at me. A few days later, I felt like throwing up again. I was glad I was safe at home where no one could see me. When I started throwing up, my mother laughed at me.

I want my mother to like me so I better not throw up again.

One day, I started playing the piano. I could not read music so I made it up as I went along. It sounded good and I was having fun. Then my mother came in and started laughing at me. I started throwing up again.

I switched from the piano to the violin. My violin teacher was very beautiful. I hoped that someday, if I became a famous violinist, she would fall in love with me. I went to the bathroom a lot during my violin lessons because my violin teacher hung her underwear over the bathtub.

I became bored with my violin lessons and stopped practicing. My father put my violin on a high shelf in the closet where I couldn't reach it. Then, he took me to a shop where they sold violins. The owner of the store showed us famous violins and told us stories of the famous violinists who played them. The next day, my father took me to Carnegie Hall. A violinist played a concerto with the orchestra. At the end of the concert, everyone stood up and cheered. When I got home, I stood on a chair and took my violin down from the high shelf. Then, I started practicing again.

* * *

When I was 12, I decided to see the world. I got on a bus. The fare was 25 cents. The bus went across the George Washington Bridge and into New Jersey. It traveled through towns and passed by farms and lakes. People got off at different stops. After a while, I was the only one left on the bus. The driver asked me where I was going.

"I want to go as far as I can for my 25 cents."

"This bus has an accumulating fare," said the driver. "You already owe me $13.75."

"But I only have 25 cents!"

The driver stopped the bus and called the police. My father had to drive to the middle of New Jersey to get me out of the police station.

On Sunday afternoons, my father took me and my brother Peter to visit Grandma Black. Her name was Sonia Belahovsky and she lived on West 168 Street on the edge of Harlem. She was born in Odessa and came to America on a ship that took six weeks to cross the Atlantic. My father was born on the Lower East Side of Manhattan. When he was two, my father's father went out to buy a newspaper and never returned. My father told me that when he was growing up, he used to dream of his father coming back. My father never saw his father again.

Grandma Black lived in stark contrast to Grandpa Goldmark. She owned a button shop and the rugs in her small apartment were covered with newspapers to keep them from getting dirty. She played one-sided Caruso records on an old-fashioned Victrola with scratchy noises. For lunch, Grandma Black cooked borscht made from very red beets and she served rice cakes for dessert. When my father gave my grandmother money, she put it in a jar labeled "For David's Education." Grandma Black smelled of talcum powder and it was more fun to hug her than my mother, who always seemed too busy.

After lunch with Grandma Black, my father took me and my brother to a park on the Lower East Side to throw a football around. Then, we went to the Fulton Fish Market. My father told us that New York City was built on concrete and all the food New Yorkers ate had to be brought in at night by trucks. My father asked strangers how they felt about life. When someone wanted money, my father offered to buy them a meal instead. We ate with some odd characters, but I was proud to be the son of someone who knew how to talk to strangers.

When we got home, my mother was usually angry. I could not figure out if she was annoyed because she had to delay supper, or for some other reason. She often complained of migraine headaches and said she wasn't feeling well, which made me want to stay home and take care of her.

My mother taught English and worked on low-cost housing studies for the poor, but at home she did not seem happy. At the dining table, she never got a chance to talk, and sometimes it seemed as though she was tiptoeing around the house herself. When I did things she didn't approve of, my mother asked Peter, "What should we do with him?" I did not think my brother was the right person to ask.

In contrast to my mother's moods and headaches, my father enjoyed his work. In between his Sunday talks, he fought for better housing for minority groups and volunteered to improve anti-discrimination laws. He also counseled young girls who were pregnant. At dinner, my father told us about interesting people he met like Vice President Henry Wallace. Whenever my father performed a wedding, he told us he had fallen in love with the bride. I wondered what my mother was thinking.

* * *

One Saturday afternoon, my friend's father took us to the Ringling Bros. and Barnum & Bailey Circus. It was called *The Greatest Show on Earth!* I found myself in Madison Square Garden, watching elephants, tigers, clowns, and acrobats. High overhead, trapeze artists performed daring feats while a loud band played. When one of the trapeze artists was about to fly through the air there was a loud drum roll, which only stopped when he was safely in the hands of another trapeze artist who was hanging upside down on a swing to catch him.

The stars of *The Greatest Show on Earth!* were the lion tamer, the tightrope walker, and a clown named Felix Adler. Felix Adler was also the name of the founder of the Ethical Culture Society.

I decided to star in a show called "The Greatest Show off Earth!" I consulted with my grandfather who said I could use his study for my stage and the sliding doors as a curtain to separate it from the audience in the living room.

I produced "The Greatest Show off Earth!" in "Grandpa's Square Garden." The audience consisted of my parents, my grandparents, and their cook and maid.

I began the "The Greatest Show off Earth!" with an overture played on my violin, and followed it with some opening words. Then, I delivered an address on how to obtain peace in the world, and I ended with a song and some closing words. When Peter closed the sliding doors to enthusiastic applause, I knew I had taken my first step towards an important destiny.

* * *

One day, my father told me he had a dream of a camp where young people would go to learn to become good citizens. He said he was going to speak to Eleanor Roosevelt about it. Two weeks later, when I came home from school, Eleanor Roosevelt was sitting in our living room listening to my father. Mrs. Roosevelt was the most famous woman in the world. She had the same first name as my mother but spelled it differently, and she looked happy and at home sitting on our couch. Mrs. Roosevelt liked my father's idea and together they started the Encampment for Citizenship, which became the forerunner of the Peace Corps.

I went to The Ethical Culture School where they taught the boys to cook and the girls to play ice hockey. When we were making the "cheese dreams," I put them in the broiler instead of the oven. My teacher made me serve up the little heaps of ashes to each of my classmates. When I didn't run fast enough, my gym teacher kicked me. But I was proud of my school because one of its graduates had invented the atomic bomb.

"Use your summers to have meaningful experiences that will enrich your life," said my father. He got me a job as a dishwasher. My feet became swollen from standing in the same place. The next summer, he found a job for me cutting brush for the electric company. I got hay fever. Then, my father arranged for me to work as a counselor for kids who had never been to camp. One of them attacked me with a knife. I went to a camp where they meditated every day. I meditated about the girl sitting next to me.

My father had a secretary named Linda with long red hair. She played the piano in our living room. She smoked and coughed and talked in a husky voice. My father said she had left her husband in Philadelphia. When Linda played the piano, the smell of her perfume, combined with the cigarette smoke, traveled down the hall and into my room when I was trying to get to sleep.

"How do you make love to a woman?"

"When two people fall in love," said my father, "they lie down and hold each other very tightly. Then, it just happens. If you ever want to do it come to me and I will arrange it."

One weekend, Linda stayed with us in our country home in Rhinebeck. On the way home in the car, I reached over and held her hand. She didn't take it away. When we got home, I told my father I wanted to make love to Linda and I asked him to arrange it. My father never answered me.

One evening, my grandfather sang a beautiful song at the dining room table. He told me it was "The Prize Song" from an opera called *Die Meistersinger von Nurnberg* by Richard Wagner. Then he took me to see *Die Meistersinger* at the Met. The Metropolitan Opera House was the biggest place I had ever seen, and during the intermission, my grandfather took me backstage. It was exciting to see the opera singers in their makeup and costumes up close. They were real people who knew how to become other people the minute the curtain went up. And when they sang, it was even more magical. I decided to become an opera singer.

When I was 15, I grew a mustache and got a job as an extra at the Met. I marched behind some horses and carried a spear. The man next to me had never been on a stage before. When we marched up some steps to a platform, he kept staring at the audience. He marched off the end of the platform and fell into the orchestra pit. In another opera, the tenor was supposed to die onstage in a sword fight. Another man and I had to carry him off on a stretcher. The other man went right and I went left. We banged the "dead" tenor against the scenery. He jumped off the stretcher and yelled at me in a foreign language.

In another opera, I stood behind a piece of scenery in a big crowd scene and waved a handkerchief. My grandfather was sitting in the audience and he told me he could see my hand waving the handkerchief. When the music was at its loudest, I sang a few notes. Then, I told all my friends I had sung at the Met.

I decided I was going to have an exciting career singing at the Met. All I needed was a big voice. My grandfather arranged singing lessons for me with a voice teacher named Clyde Burrows, who had been a professional baseball player. He began my first lesson by telling me that opera singers needed strong stomach muscles. Then, he told me to punch him in the stomach. I hit him as hard as I could and hurt my hand. Burrows told me to start throwing my voice out of the window. I hoped that one day I would be able to turn my punching and shouting into operatic arias.

* * *

My father taught ethics at the Ethical Culture Fieldston School. On Sundays he was God, and on Thursdays he was Socrates. I was doing well in English and German, but failing to make the grade socially. Fieldston was no longer The School for Working Men's Children started by Felix Adler. Times had changed since Grandma Black had first sought it out as a haven for my father after a teacher slammed his head against a blackboard in a public school. The high tuition that helped pay for the teachers and the upkeep of the elaborate grounds meant that most of the students came from wealthy Jewish families. I was one of three students in my class on a scholarship, which I received because I was the son of Algernon Black. Being without money was a major handicap. Most of the students drove their own cars and gave expensive parties. One of my classmates handed out cash to everyone who came to his birthday party.

I was too small for the football team and as the son of a teacher, I was eyed with suspicion by the other students, so I was not a candidate for the social mainstream. This was not a new feeling. When I was born, my parents were living near Gramercy Park but they did not have a key to get into it. As a child I watched other children in the park through the iron entrance gate wondering why I was not allowed to play with them.

The show business aspects of Ethical Culture were easy to recognize in my father's fire and brimstone talks on Sunday mornings. But behind the theatrics, there was something deeper, something of greater substance that was more elusive. At the Ethical Culture Fieldston School, as a member of the underclass, I was beginning to experience the anger and injustice that fueled my father's sermons. My father's authority to challenge the capitalist system came from not being part of it. That's where he found his strength and his opportunity. If I was going to follow in my father's footsteps, I would have to find my own cause to champion.

I began campaigning for reform in the student government. I made speeches before the student council about the lack of student representation and other ills. Even though there were only three have-nots in my class, including myself, I discovered there was a group of them in each of the other five grades that made up the school.

Here was a power bloc that could propel me into contention for the school's highest office. The position of president of the student council automatically made the honored recipient president of his class and the school as well. This exalted post lasted for the entire senior year of one lucky student. I spent my junior year campaigning for it.

With the support of all the underprivileged students at the Ethical Culture Fieldston School, I became one of the three candidates for president of the student council. The favorite to win was the tallest in our class and a conspicuous member of the "in" crowd.

"Expect to lose," said my father. "That way you won't be disappointed when you *do* lose."

Our last pre-election act was to write a piece for the school newspaper that would appear under our respective photographs. To save money, I had my picture taken in a penny arcade. The photograph came out with a black border around it. When my photograph was printed in the school newspaper, it looked like my obituary.

I won!

It wasn't clear whether the students voted for me out of sympathy or because they didn't like the conspicuous member of the in crowd. To some the black border around my photograph suggested I had found the courage to face my mortality. In any case, I had won the election!

To celebrate, I went to dinner with my father and Linda in a restaurant on Times Square and to a movie at the Capitol Theatre.

Where is my mother? This is the most important moment of my life and she isn't here!

After the film, I stood at the top of the Capitol's steps and thanked my father and Linda with an acceptance speech. For one brief and glorious moment, Ethical Culture had paid off and put me on a pedestal all my own.

"Stay Away from the Upper Class!"

"You can go to a small college and be a big fish in a little pond," said my father, "or you can go to a big college and be a little fish in a big pond." I wanted to go to a big college and be a big fish in a big pond. The big college I wanted to go to was Harvard because both my father and my grandfather had gone there, but the Ethical Culture Fieldston School was under a quota system, which meant Harvard would only accept four members of our senior class. Eight of my classmates applied to Harvard and out of our group, four had perfect scores on the SATs. I was not one of them. To be one of the select four to go to Harvard, I would have to have something in addition to relatives who were graduates.

Harvard was looking for students with extracurricular credits, in addition to academic skills, and I hoped that being president of the school and my class qualified. I sent in my application and waited patiently for a reply. One day it came. I had been accepted! I ran into the living room to tell my parents. While they were congratulating me, my brother Peter had a big smile on his face because he had written the letter.

In spite of Peter, I got into Harvard. My grandfather rewarded me with an invitation to join my grandparents at their favorite resort in Canada, which featured two lodges on a lake. One of the lodges was for "Newly Weds" and the other was for "Nearly Deads." My grandparents stayed in the "Nearly Deads." Alone amongst the "Newly Weds," I met an unhappily married housewife. She told me I had "bedroom eyes" and invited me to join her in bed. I was not prepared to take full advantage of this opportunity because, at 17, I was still a stranger to the mysteries of lovemaking.

I didn't know what to do. I held her tightly as my father had advised but nothing happened. Nevertheless, the lonely lady showered me with gifts and wrote me letters. Having an older woman in love with me was an accomplishment, and I proudly showed her letters to my father.

"Never let a woman get her hooks into you," said my father.

I wondered if my mother ever got her hooks into my father. My father unhooked me from the Canadian housewife by writing a goodbye letter to her, and getting me to sign it. God had rescued me from my love life.

* * *

The big pond of Harvard seemed more like an ocean. Out of my freshman class of 1,000, I only knew three of my classmates because they came from Fieldston. But then an opportunity presented itself. The president of Harvard, James Bryant Conant, invited all the freshmen to tea in the presidential mansion. I decided to reciprocate, and I invited the president for drinks in my room. No president of Harvard had ever been invited for drinks by a freshman. President Conant came with his wife and the event was written up in the *Harvard Crimson*. My friends told me to take advantage of the publicity and run for president of the class. I hired a parrot and I taught it to say, "David Black for president!" Then I took the parrot to the freshman dining room during lunch. The parrot was nervous in front of so many people. It sat on its perch and didn't say anything. When the parrot finally started to say, "David Black for president!" it shat all over the table. I lost the election.

My father had waited on tables in the very hall where I was now eating. He filled me with tales of the privileged "upper" class at Harvard, and how wealthy families paid for accommodations where their fortunate offspring could live with their lady friends. This area was called The Gold Coast, and presumably did not exist anymore, but the traditions of upper-class Harvardians continued.

One of my classmates told me about a sophomore named Bill Perry who wanted to be an opera conductor. His father gave him an annual birthday present of an orchestra, chorus, and soloists to conduct. This year, he was using his birthday present to conduct a production of Johann Strauss's operetta *The Gypsy Baron*. The well-known Polish soprano Polyna Stoska had just been kicked out of the Met and Perry had recruited her to sing the lead. The rest of the cast was unknown, including a singing actor named Fred Gwynne, who later went on to star in the TV comedy *The Munsters*. I auditioned for the role of Pali, the head knife-wielding gypsy, and got the part. My voice lessons with Clyde Burrows had paved the way for my first extracurricular activity at Harvard. I was about to swim in the ocean.

* * *

At the first rehearsal of *The Gypsy Baron,* I met a young woman who was a dancer in the chorus. Her name was Linda but she didn't smoke or play the piano. I followed her home on my bicycle. Linda's last name was Cabot, which meant nothing to me except it did not sound Jewish. She was a junior at Radcliffe and was three years older than me. Linda was living in a cozy rented room with a fireplace in an old house in Cambridge and she was majoring in music. We found we shared a love of music that went beyond *The Gypsy Baron*. Linda seemed interested when I described my experiences at the Met as an extra. She listened intently as I told her about my grandfather and his uncle, Karl Goldmark, who had composed the opera *The Queen of Sheba*, which held the record for the most performances in one season at the Met. On another evening, I brought a recording of Goldmark's Violin Concerto and we listened to its beautiful Hungarian melodies. We rode our bicycles to *The Gypsy Baron* rehearsals and chained them together. We blended our voices rehearsing the music by Johann Strauss, another composer from the fabled city of Vienna, where Karl Goldmark had been a drinking companion of Johannes Brahms.

I started thinking about *The Gypsy Baron* rehearsals while I was attending classes, but my thoughts were no longer centered on Polyna Stoska. During rehearsals, I found myself looking at Linda whenever the tenor sang, "There's a world on a string, if you're young and alone. You can live like a king, if your heart is your own."

I told Linda about my search for musical gods to help me express my feelings and we shared our admiration for Richard Wagner. I had attended his *Ring* cycle at the Met, where I stood in line for hours to buy a ticket for the right to stand for more hours at each of his operas. We listened to *Tristan and Isolde* in front of the fire and as the music of the *Liebestod* surrounded the crackling flames, Tristan's longings became mine.

When I mentioned Linda to one of my classmates, he told me the Cabots were a famous family. He said they were considered the ultimate bluebloods of Boston and to prove it he recited a poem: "Here's to Boston, the land of the bean and the cod, where the Lowells speak only to the Cabots and the Cabots speak only to God."

The news of Linda's exalted upper-class status inspired me to action. I began championing my father's causes. I described how he was devoting his life to helping the poor and minorities by fighting for their rights, and I recited the litany of Ethical Culture as if it were my own: "Man makes his own hell or heaven on this earth. There is no God who will solve the problems of the world!" Ethical Culture had become the white horse on which I hoped to ride into the upper-class world that my father had warned me to stay away from. The Cabots were Wagner's Ring of Fire surrounding the Walküre rock, which protected the sleeping bride I hoped to carry off.

After a few months, Linda invited me to meet her parents. My father had told me the best way to recognize an anti-Semite was when someone said, "Some of my best friends are Jews." We drove up a long driveway to a medium-sized mansion. Linda's parents were standing on the front lawn.

"I'm happy to meet you," said Linda's father, Tom Cabot. "Some of my best friends are Jews."

During lunch, Linda's father told me the family spent a lot of time fox-hunting, white-water canoeing, sailing, and riding horses over mountains. He invited me on a fox hunt. Tom Cabot loaned me a pair of riding boots, riding pants, a black-and-white vest, a hard hat, and a riding crop. I felt as if I had joined a secret society and was about to go on a very important mission. After I got dressed, I had my picture taken on a horse to send to my parents.

The fox hunt began with everyone riding through the woods, as the hounds trotted along next to us. Suddenly, a fox ran under my horse, and I took off after it. I planned to jump off my horse, grab the fox, and present it to my fiancé. My horse became excited and started to gallop. I had never been on a galloping horse. My only experience with horses had been on pony rides at the Central Park Zoo. I tried to stop my horse but he just went faster. Trees were flying by and I had to duck to avoid the branches. Ahead of me was a huge stone wall. I could feel my horse gathering himself for a mighty leap. I hung on for dear life. As I sailed over the wall, I passed the rest of the hunt in mid-air going in the opposite direction.

"No one is allowed over a jump ahead of the master of hounds," said Tom Cabot. "You have been expelled from the hunt!"

* * *

"There is only one thing to remember in white-water canoeing," said Tom Cabot. "If you tip over, never let the canoe come between you and the current. If that happens you will drown, and lose the canoe."

Sitting in the stern of our canoe, with Linda in the bow, I could see more Cabots, including her parents and brothers, paddling canoes in front of us. The river was calm and so was I. I was eager to redeem myself after fox hunting and this seemed the ideal sport since I had spent three summers canoeing on a lake at the Ethical Culture School Camp. As we rounded a bend in the river, the water started to bubble and rocks began to appear. Then, I heard a low rumbling sound. I could see the heads of more Cabots ahead of us as the front of our canoe tipped downwards and we went over a waterfall.

Before I knew it, we had bumped and splashed our way to the bottom of the falls. Members of the family who had negotiated the falls were pulling up to the river bank where a picnic lunch was laid out.

They were watching us and I felt proud that we had come through unscathed. Just at this moment, I saw the branch of a tree sticking out from the shore. I tried to avoid it but we were moving too swiftly, and in one fleeting moment our canoe flipped over. My glasses flew off and I began swallowing water. Linda had disappeared. I didn't want to lose the canoe in full view of the family so I held on to it. I realized I was in the exact position Tom Cabot had warned me about. I could feel the canoe pushing against me with the force of the current behind it. I was being forced down in the water. I let go of the canoe and it flew over my head. I swam to the bank and climbed up. I was soaking wet and I did not have the canoe, my glasses, or Linda. The Cabots were eating lunch and didn't seem concerned.

Although I was not officially engaged to Linda, my experiences were beginning to feel like trials to earn that privilege. I was like Tamino in Mozart's *The Magic Flute*, but instead of singing arias to win the bride, I was fighting my way out of life-threatening situations. After the canoeing debacle, I wondered if I would ever be invited to join the Cabots again. Then, an invitation arrived from Tom Cabot to join them on the family yacht.

How much trouble could I get into sailing? All I have to do is to stay out of the way.

The Cabot boat on which I was to make my maiden voyage was called *Avelinde*, named after the lady I was unofficially courting, and it was moored in the Chesapeake Bay in Maryland to escape the harsh New England winters. Linda and I joined her parents for a weekend cruise on their 60-foot yawl. My plan was to do as little as possible since I knew the Cabots were legendary sailors. Tom told me the family was descended from Giovanni Caboto, the famous sailor who had discovered America before Columbus. In addition to this impressive fact, Linda and her mother had sailed *Avelinde* all by themselves in the Atlantic during World War II.

Lying in the sun on *Avelinde's* deck as she moved gently through the waters, I was pleased that my passenger status had been accepted with nothing expected of me. Tom was at the helm and Linda was in the galley, preparing lunch with her mother. Then Tom suggested I climb up the steps on the main mast to what looked like a little basket. He said it was called the crow's nest and I would enjoy the view. Climbing the steps was easy enough, and up I went. Once I arrived at the lofty perch, I sat down in the basket to gaze out at the water. When I looked down, however, the comfort of the deck seemed far away. I was not aware how high I had climbed and what seemed like gentle rocking when I was down below now felt like a full-force gale.

It was all I could do to hold on to the mast as it swayed back and forth. I descended as quickly as I could without revealing my fright and climbed safely into the little rowboat that *Avelinde* was towing.

The water looked inviting and we were barely moving so I decided to jump in and hold on to the back of the rowboat. In case I lost my grip, I tied the rowboat's rope around one of my legs. While I was hanging on to the rowboat, enjoying the sun and the feel of the water, *Avelinde's* motor suddenly started and the boat hurtled forward. I lost my grip on the rowboat and found myself being dragged backwards through the water. I yelled to Tom, but he was busy turning the boat in a new direction. As *Avelinde's* speed increased, I was pulled under the water with the rope still around my leg. As water filled my mouth, making it impossible to breathe, I realized I was being "keel-hauled," a punishment reserved for bad sailors, which usually resulted in death. I fought against the speed of the water by tightening my stomach muscles and I was finally able to sit up. As I threw myself into the rowboat, I realized I was right. Tom Cabot did not want me to join the family.

* * *

Since Linda was the only female Cabot available for marriage, competition for her hand was heating up. She had made her debut into Boston society with a different kind of coming-out party. Instead of the customary formal affair at one of Boston's leading hotels, the Cabots had put on a party with a Bavarian theme in one of their country retreats. All the young men had worn lederhosen and the women had appeared in Austrian dress. There had been an oompah band and dancing. The party signaled the opening of the marriage hunting season. Boston's eligible bachelors from all the right families had set their sights on this Cabot prize.

Although I was not seriously contemplating marriage, I was intrigued by the challenge of competing. Once again, I was the underdog. This time, however, the stakes were higher than becoming president of the student council. If I married a woman from the upper class, I was sure to earn my father's permanent disappointment.

I was not the only one to reject what my family wanted. Linda was also in revolt against her father and the traditions he represented. She had grown up in a male-dominated family with three older brothers, and although she enjoyed Cabot horses, sailboats, chalets, and ranches, she needed to put her personal stamp of identity on whatever she could. Living off campus, studying music, performing in operettas, and requesting an unorthodox coming-out party were just the beginning. Now, she had found an even better way to rebel against her family's lifestyle. Consorting with a Jewish intellectual from New York was a poisonous arrow she could launch in her father's direction that might have lethal results. Our destinies had joined. Our attraction for each other would not only be the basis for a happy life together, it would make it possible for both of us to clobber our fathers.

By now it was obvious to both Linda and me that fox hunting, white-water canoeing, and sailing were not fruitful activities for me to pursue; that left waltzing. On Friday nights, in Boston's Ritz Hotel, white-gloved, formally clad young men waltzed the objects of their wooing around the ballroom floor to strains of a famous orchestra, while their proper Bostonian relatives gazed approvingly from the sidelines. But no such approving glances would be coming our way. In fact, the only thing standing in the way of my success as the Rhett Butler of New York in this New England *Gone with the Wind* was the problem that I could only waltz in one direction. When the rest of the field reversed, Linda and I kept on going.

While Linda reveled in my inability to conform to the traditions of Boston society, I began to feel inadequate. With all the attention I had been paying to her, my academic work had descended to the level of a gentleman's C mixed with a few Ds. I was even relying on Linda to help me with some of my homework, so I could find more time for extracurricular activities. This would have been all right if I had something exciting to show for my efforts. But the only thing I managed to win was the lead in another student operetta, and neither the Cabots nor the Blacks came to see it.

Being in show business at Harvard was not as impressive as it might have been elsewhere. This ivy-covered institution was preparing young men to run corporations, law firms, and the country itself. Harvard students were getting ready to make their mark in the world as doctors, scientists, and lawyers, not as opera singers.

I could not think of a dramatic way to prove my right to the prize I had been pursuing, but as luck would have it, Tom Cabot himself paved the way for the final chapter by appearing unannounced at the Ethical Culture Society in New York.

"Your son is trying to get his hands on my daughter's money!" Tom Cabot bellowed to my father. "What are you going to do about it?"

My father immediately realized this upper-class Boston Brahmin was the perfect partner to help him stop me from marrying into the upper class. He invited Tom Cabot to breakfast, and several days later I learned the results of their meeting. Linda told me her parents had suggested she join them on her own for a cruise on *Avelinde*. After four days, Linda jumped ship and called me. We spent the evening strolling along the Charles River. Under one of its bridges, I heard myself saying, "You know, you are the kind of girl boys like me end up marrying." I didn't know it but I had just uttered a proposal of marriage.

* * *

My next problem was how to finance the purchase of an engagement ring. My personal finances were nonexistent and my valuable possessions consisted of Dixie-cup tops and rocks I had collected in Central Park. Once again, my grandfather came to my rescue. I sold the stamp collection he had given me as a gift when I left for Harvard and made $200, enough to purchase a ring. Linda and I decided that after our wedding, we would live in Europe, where I could pursue my operatic career in Italy, the birthplace of opera.

Our engagement party was to be held in the family home where Tom Cabot first told me that some of his best friends were Jews. Upper-class sisters, cousins, and aunts were summoned from Beacon Hill and board meetings and embassies to meet the Cabots' future Jewish son-in-law.

There were very few skills I felt confident about in the presence of my future in-laws; on the day of the party, I was on the lookout for something I could do that would make a favorable impression. Linda's mother discovered there were dead goldfish at the bottom of the pool in the garden where the party was to take place. I gallantly whipped off my pants and waded into the pool in my undershorts. As I emerged from the pool, carrying the dead goldfish, Linda's mother introduced me to each of my future Cabot relatives so they wouldn't mistake me for the caretaker.

At the engagement party, congratulations were showered on us by the cream of Boston society, including Senator Henry Cabot Lodge, Jr. I was filled with the satisfaction of a deed well done. The courting of Linda had ended and I had won the prize. Linda's brothers seemed content and so did her former beaus, some of whom had been invited.

The effect of being welcomed into the bosom of the Cabot family was to hasten the next step, which was not what Tom Cabot had in mind. Now, there could be no backing down; Linda and her mother began planning the wedding.

The first decision to be made was who would perform the ceremony. I automatically thought of my father, who, as a leader of the Ethical Culture Society, had performed many weddings. Even though I was marrying against my father's will into a family of wealth and privilege, I wanted him to officiate. This would be my way of competing against the formidable array of Cabot accomplishments. However, because Linda's uncle was Rev. Palfrey Perkins, the minister of King's Chapel in Boston where the Cabots spoke only to God, we decided we should have a joint ceremony — performed by my father and Linda's uncle.

Three months into my junior year and one month after my 19th birthday, Linda and I were married in front of several hundred guests in the Cabots' family church near their home in Weston, Massachusetts. The ushers were a Cabot, a Lowell, a Lodge, and my roommates: a Goodman, a Rosenman, and a Halberstam, proving that at least half of Tom Cabot's best friends were Jews.

Before the ceremony was about to begin, Rev. Palfrey Perkins put on purple and black robes, which were elaborately decorated in gold. My father turned pale and gave me a disapproving look. Ethical Culture did not approve of the robes of ritual. For a moment, I was concerned my father might not go through with the ceremony, but then he joined Rev. Perkins at the altar just as Tom Cabot began to march down the aisle with Linda on his arm. The procession was led by Linda's sisters-in-law and her classmates as bridesmaids. The long white train of her ancient family wedding dress was held by two eight-year-old pages, Linda's younger brother Ned, and my younger brother Jonathan.

After Rev. Perkins administered the church's traditional marriage vows, he nodded to my father, who said, "It is traditional to call down a blessing on you. But I say, bless you one another. It is your love that gives this marriage a promise of happiness and the power to work out a good life together. May you never rob each other of the taste for life and may your joys be greater because you share them together."

While my father was saying these words, I remembered how I stood in line for the first time to shake his hand after his Sunday talk at the Ethical Culture Society. My father had asked me if he was any good. I was embarrassed and I didn't know what to say. Now, performing his marriage ceremony for the bluebloods of Boston I was proud of him. And I hoped he was proud of me, even though I was now a member of the upper class.

* * *

After our honeymoon, I moved into Linda's basement apartment in Cambridge. My plan was to finish my junior year as quickly as possible and then attend Harvard's summer school, where I could pick up enough credits to graduate a year early. In my search for ever easier courses, I found one where it wasn't necessary to read any books, or attend any classes. All I had to do was write a paper about something. I decided to write about the techniques I was learning in the acting class I was taking at the Brattle Theater along with two classmates, Fred Gwynne from *The Gypsy Baron*, and an aspiring actor named Jack Lemmon. At our first class, the instructor told us to write down all the sounds we could hear. Then, he told us to close our eyes and listen again. We heard more sounds with our eyes closed. I was hoping that learning to act would help me to become an opera singer.

To prepare for my operatic career, I appeared as a soloist with the Harvard Glee Club as often as possible. My new voice teacher was Ruth Streeter, who gave me free lessons in return for letting her try to convert me to Christian Science. Instead of throwing my voice out the window with Clyde Burrows, I was learning a new version of Ethical Culture.

Because I was a soloist with the Harvard Glee Club, I was offered a scholarship to sing in the opera department at Tanglewood with the Boston Symphony Orchestra. The scholarship included private voice lessons with Hugh Ross, who prepared the Tanglewood chorus to sing with the Boston Symphony. "Vibrato is the key to a great voice," said Ross. While I was singing, he took hold of my Adam's apple and wiggled it back and forth in time to a metronome.

In addition to free lessons with Hugh Ross, the other benefit of my Tanglewood scholarship was to appear in a small role in Jacques Ibert's *The King of Ivetot*, the summer production of the Tanglewood Opera Company. The leading roles were played by Mario Lanza and George London. Singing even a few notes on the same stage with these opera greats was an inspiring experience.

After graduating Harvard in three years, I was free to pursue my operatic dream. Most successful American opera singers started their careers in Europe. My wife was supporting me, but at least I would be doing it 3,000 miles from home.

Because Linda controlled the purse strings, I was subject to her frugality. If I had my way, we would have sailed to Europe on the fanciest liner afloat, but New England thriftiness won out and we made the voyage on a German freight ship with ten passengers. In

September of 1953, we boarded the S.S. *Spreewald* in the Brooklyn Navy Yard. We were shown to our cabin next to the boiler room. There was no way I could express my unhappiness to Linda without appearing to look a gift horse in the mouth.

As the S.S. *Spreewald* sailed out of New York Harbor, I thought about my parents. I had defied my father by marrying into the upper class. Now I was going to Europe to become an opera singer. When I returned, my voice would be bigger than his. My mother would have to listen.

Learning to "Singa" the High Notes

The good ship *Spreewald* took 12 days to cross the Atlantic and it was manned by personnel who looked suspiciously like representatives of Hitler's Third Reich. During the voyage, I played chess with the first mate who became angry when I won. I had started playing chess at the age of eight when my father matched me up with old men on stone benches in Central Park. This experience had come in handy when I learned that my new father-in-law played chess, but whenever I was about to win a game from Tom Cabot, I found myself thinking about fox hunting, canoeing, and sailing. Then I made a mistake and lost the game. When the captain of the *Spreewald* heard that I defeated the first mate in chess, he challenged me to a game. Alone in the middle of the Atlantic Ocean, I was feeling my Jewishness. If I won, the captain might throw me overboard or clap me in irons. While I was thinking these thoughts, I made a mistake and lost the game.

On the *Spreewald*, there were two breakfasts, one lunch, and then tea followed by dinner, making five meals in all. The aroma of German cooking mixed with the fragrant sea air as we approached the land of Bach, Beethoven, Mozart, Brahms, and Wagner. Linda had been to Europe when she was seven years old on a grand tour with her family, but I had only been there in my dreams. The excitement was building before our first sight of land. No Mayflower ancestor of Linda's or Giovanni Caboto himself could have felt the excitement I now experienced. For me, the old world was new and full of promise for the future.

* * *

The *Spreewald* docked in Hamburg and Linda and I took a train to Rome, where I answered an ad promising free advice for opera singers. I found myself sitting opposite a Dr. Scuri, who wore a white coat and had a large mirror attached to his forehead. He heated up a small mirror over a candle and stuck it down my throat.

"*Tu sei tenore!*"

"How do you know I am a tenor?"

"Everybody has a two vocal chords," said Scuri. "Their length dependa on the size of your body. If you are tall, your *chordi vocali* are long and you are a bass. If you are short, your *chordi vocali* are short and you are a *tenore!*"

"This is amazing news!" I told Dr. Scuri. "But I have never sung above an F-sharp!"

Scuri took out a prescription form and wrote down *Tenore*. "Take this to Rachele Maragliano Mori, de best voicea teacher in *tutta Roma!* She will teach you to singa the high notes!"

When I handed Rachele Maragliano Mori the prescription from Dr. Scuri, she went to work. She began by telling me to sing as high as I could in a falsetto voice, breathing air across my vocal chords. Before I knew it, I was making a sound on high C and even on a D above it. Then, we began working our way down the scale, treating the F-sharp as though it were the middle of my vocal range.

While I was learning to "singa the high notes" with Rachele Maragliano Mori, Linda and I moved into Palazzo Taverna, the oldest palazzo in Rome. Our apartment belonged to Lida Fleitmann Bloodgood, who lived in the penthouse of the palazzo. Mrs. Bloodgood had grown up with horses in Smithtown, Long Island, where she had been Master of Hounds, a profession with which I was already acquainted. She had left her husband in an institution for alcoholics and moved to Rome with her daughter just before World War II. After the war, Mrs. Bloodgood's daughter married Prince Radziwill and moved to his farm in South Africa.

Mrs. Bloodgood had ridden horses in front of all the crowned heads of Europe and she was a friend of the pope. She was the author of a book called *Hoofs in the Distance* and she had broken almost every bone in her body. At lunch, one of her eyebrows fell off in the soup.

I was relieved to learn that jumping over fences on a horse in pursuit of a fox eventually led to physical decrepitude. Mrs. Bloodgood had an aging lover, Major Piero Santini, with whom she coauthored a book about the Italian forward seat in horseback riding, even though Mrs. Bloodgood always rode sidesaddle. She also had a cook named Ludovica and a dachshund named Picci.

Lunch took place on Mrs. Bloodgood's wisteria-covered terrace overlooking the rooftops of Rome with the river Tiber and the Castel Sant'Angelo in the distance. The meal began with a pasta called *malfatti*, which means "badly made." It consisted of spinach and pasta dough cooked and rolled together in a butter sauce with cheese on top. Ludovica served us herself, flopping about in slippers with the tops cut off to accommodate her oversized feet. She looked like an overweight opera singer and I realized if I went on eating her food, I might become a Walküre myself. This did not bother me because all great opera singers were fat, which obviously had something to do with their vocal prowess. Maybe the extra weight from eating *malfatti* would increase the thickness of my vocal chords and Dr. Scuri would pronounce me a dramatic tenor, which would mean I could sing Siegfried.

* * *

Rome was a city with no middle class. It was inhabited by movie stars, clergy, titled nobility, and the extremely poor. Palazzo Taverna was located in the middle of the poorest section near the church where Mario Cavaradossi painted his famous portrait of Tosca in the opera of the same name. Nobility was still a Roman way of life, as in Caesar's day, and beautifully adorned ladies emerged from the tenements surrounding Palazzo Taverna as if they were titled princesses. Even the poor were beautifully dressed.

In addition to churches and movie stars, Romans were in love with eating. This major pastime took so long during the middle of the day that one required a siesta afterward to recover. Eating began again in the late evening and took the place of theatrical entertainments, which were few. Restaurants abounded and Linda and I began researching them and their dishes. At Pipernos in the Jewish quarter, we feasted on fried artichokes. At a small restaurant below the Spanish steps we consumed four-layered fried sandwiches, and at a nearby Hungarian nightclub we ate spaghetti Hungarian-style while violins played. On Piazza Novona we indulged in chewy chocolate ice cream, and at Il Pompiere we had veal dishes with pasta on the side. This restaurant had been financed by a famous female opera singer who craved a big meal and the attentions of her boyfriend immediately after every performance. Her boyfriend was a fireman, hence the name Pompiere, and photos of the two of them eating together hung on the walls. If operatic success depended on weight, I stood a good chance of succeeding. When we arrived in Rome, I weighed 140 pounds. Now, after almost a year, I was up to 190 and my neck had disappeared.

Several times a week, I wrote postcards to my grandfather, providing him with details of my operatic progress. I also sent him photographs, hoping he would see that I looked more like a tenor with my added weight. My grandfather once told me, "Some people eat to live and others live to eat." He was proud to be among those who lived to eat. He was particularly fond of the chicken pot pie at the Lawyers Club and the popovers at the Harvard Club. Once, he invited my cousin and me to the Harmonie Club and pitted us against each other in a contest to see who could eat the most new potatoes. I won by eating 22. It was important that my grandfather be kept informed of my experiences. It was almost as important as the experiences themselves.

As we began 1955 in the City of Seven Hills, it was hard to tell what progress I was actually making. Mori had succeeded in teaching me to sing up to a high C, but it seemed to me I had lost some of the power to project my voice, which I had when I was a baritone. Of course, I had no way of knowing how I would actually sound in a large opera house. In spite of my doubts, Mori said she was pleased with my progress and I decided to take her word for it.

While I was pursuing my operatic career, Linda was studying Dante and reading his poems in Italian. She was also attending exhibitions in Rome's amazing museums and urging me to join her. I was feeling sluggish because of my added weight. I found it difficult to wake up in the morning and even more difficult after my afternoon siesta. The heavy *malfatti* lunches on Mrs. Bloodgood's terrace made my voice lower when I woke up. Instead of attending museums, I had to exercise for over an hour before I was ready to "singa the high notes." Then I traveled to my singing lessons on the streetcar in the late afternoon, listening to American seminarians in robes discussing parties and girls. They were unaware that I could understand every word they were saying.

The hot wind of the African sirocco blew over Rome in the late afternoon, as it had for centuries. The fact that I was not earning any money preyed on my mind. I was able to find work dubbing Italian films into English, for which I was paid 25 dollars in lire per day. Mouthing the words of Raf Vallone while he was seducing Brigitte

Bardot was sexy and it reminded me of another boyhood ambition, to be a movie star. I would have to stick with opera singing for the moment.

The news that my father had been invited to India by Pandit Nehru and planned to visit us on the way reminded me that I hadn't done anything that compared with his accomplishments. Still, I wanted to see him. When my parents told me that they had also been invited to Israel as a guest of The American Fund for Israeli Institutions, I decided to accompany them on their trip to India and Israel.

Lacking anything of substance with which to impress my parents, I ordered Curry #3 at our first Indian breakfast in Bombay while my parents had bacon and eggs. The immediate effect of this demonstration of international sophistication was a devastating stomachache. My father had the address of a doctor who was an Ethical Culture School graduate living in Bombay. The doctor pre-scribed opium and I got the medicine from the drugstore and took my first dose. It was only afterward that I read the label, which said "For External Use Only." I lay on my bed in the hotel for hours, expe-riencing an opium high. I felt as if I was being sucked up into the fan whirling over my head. At one point, I saw a sign that read "The Place Where Men Meet to Seek the Highest is Holy Ground." That evening, we attended a formal reception given by Lady Rama Rau in her palatial residence. After being introduced to her, I threw up.

After India, we continued on to Israel. Because my father believed that organized religion and its rituals were to blame for the evils of the world, he had no desire to visit Jewish synagogues, but everywhere we went, we were confronted by militant Zionists who not only believed the Jews were God's chosen people but that Israel was their sacred turf. We spoke with formerly mild-mannered New

Yorkers who had become tough and outspoken on Jewish rights, and we listened to the Israeli Philharmonic, where the violin section had trouble playing together since it was made up of former concertmasters from the leading orchestras of Europe. Feeling Jewish in the Holy Land had a strange result. During a visit to a kibbutz on the Sea of Galilee, I remembered it was the location of Christ's greatest miracle. I asked my father if he could walk on water. Without hesitation, he stepped out onto the Sea of Galilee, fully clothed, and sank.

* * *

The visit with my parents jolted me into the realization that I could not remain forever in the Eternal City. My father had not absolved me of my sins. I was still living off Linda's upper-class money and I had no job or profession. The lessons with Mori were a ritual in between orgiastic banquets of food and travel. I had begun learning the role of Rodolfo in *La Boheme* but I was nowhere near singing it. Mori's talents as a teacher were limited, and so were my vocal abilities. I made a recording of one of Rodolfo's arias while I was in the shower where there was an echo, and sent it to my grandfather. On tape, it sounded like I was already singing at the Met.

One evening, we attended a concert by the famous German singer, Dietrich Fischer-Dieskau. He sang with enormous power and beautiful phrasing. At the reception afterward, I asked him for advice. Fischer-Dieskau suggested that I study with his teacher, Hermann Weissenborn, in Berlin, who had also taught Germany's famous tenor Joseph Schmidt. "Tell Weissenborn it was my idea for you to see him," said Fischer-Dieskau.

Hermann Weissenborn was one foot shorter than me, which meant he had to stand on his toes to look into my mouth while I was singing. Dietrich Fischer-Dieskau was known for a nasal quality, which made his voice sound as though it originated in his head. This gave him a power base that helped him accomplish his famous vocal dynamics when singing. Professor Weissenborn attempted to teach me the same technique and he seemed enthusiastic about my possibilities.

Linda and I moved into a frugal room in the Charlottenburg section of West Berlin. After two years of extravagance in Rome, Linda was beginning to wonder if her would-be opera-singer husband would ever succeed. Our room was located in an apartment owned by a Dr. Hippler who gave mud baths to what seemed like most of West Berlin. The fumes from the mud, which he mixed with chemicals early in the morning, traveled down the hall and into our room. Whenever we wanted to leave the apartment, we had to slither past partially clad, out-of-shape Berliners in the hall, waiting for their turn to be submerged in Dr. Hippler's magic mud. At the end of the day, the doctor and his wife lay in the mud and invited us to join them. We courteously declined.

Dr. Hippler was also in demand for small parts in German movies because he looked like Goebbels, and he had a dramatic scar down his cheek. When I asked where he got the scar, he told me he belonged to a dueling society where members acquired scars that they would wear with pride for the rest of their lives.

Moving from Rome to Berlin was like leaving Hollywood for Detroit. The sensual outdoor life of the Romans quickly became a memory as we accustomed ourselves to vistas of endless bombed-out buildings. The beautiful Roman *campagna*, with its villas surrounding the Eternal City, was replaced by uninviting structures and a climate to match. The gloominess of Hitler's former center of power was reflected in the faces of its inhabitants and in their conversations. Shortly after we paid our first month's rent, Dr. Hippler summoned me to his office to tell me he and his wife never knew about the concentration camps.

"We were *totally* surprised when we heard about them," he said. He did not sound convincing.

On Sunday afternoons, we attended musical soirees at the home of Dietrich Fischer-Dieskau, who was producing his own version of "The Greatest Show off Earth!" He sang songs to a group of selected friends and then delivered a lecture on the meaning of music before serving dessert and coffee to his adoring disciples who sat at his feet on the living-room floor. On one of these occasions, I met Mark White, the head of the Armed Forces Radio Network for Western Germany. On hearing I was an American tenor, White suggested I record some songs for the Armed Forces Network in Berlin. He said he could play them Sunday afternoons for 15 minutes right after Frank Sinatra. *Songs by David Black* became a series of 13 Sunday radio programs and I had to add new songs to my repertoire. I put together a collection of love songs from the seventeenth and eighteenth century from Germany, Italy, and America, including a series of songs written for George Washington called "A Washington Garland."

One day Hermann Weissenborn suggested I take voice lessons from one of his pupils instead of himself. He said that way it would be cheaper and I could take more lessons. I couldn't figure out if he was trying to help me, or get rid of me. My new teacher was Brigitte Weidner, a blonde-haired blue-eyed beauty who would obviously be singing Brünnhilde one day. Brigitte's presence all by itself was enough to inspire me and I threw myself into my voice lessons with a new gusto. Linda wanted to meet Brigitte and she decided she would also take voice lessons. Whatever Linda's motive, I could not help thinking of *Everybody Does It*, a film where a self-centered opera star gives a party for herself in her apartment. The guests are suddenly amazed by an incredible singing voice coming from the shower. It turns out to be the opera star's husband who is a construction worker. The diva's agent is at the party. She dumps the diva and starts managing her husband.

One afternoon, I was nursing a beer at the popular Maison de France when two Americans in trench coats sat down at my table.

"Do you love your country?" asked a well-dressed, middle-aged man with a serious expression.

"Of course!" I replied.

"You don't know us, but we know you," said the other man. "Because you are a student of voice in Berlin with your own radio program and because you speak German without an American accent, you are in a position to do something very important for the American people."

The men told me they were with the CIA and they wanted me to work for them. They had been doing research for several months and had enough information on me, the Blacks, and the Cabots to convince me their credentials were authentic. Although I would not be paid a salary, I would receive money for room and board.

It took me a few moments to realize I was not starring in a movie and this was not "The CIA scene." The agents greeted my stunned silence with the assurance that working for the agency would make me feel like a patriot.

"You will be proud of the contribution you will be making to the welfare of the United States," said the man with the serious expression.

The thought of becoming the Tokyo Rose of Berlin thrilled me to the core. At last, I would go legit. No Black or Cabot would be able to match my heroic deeds.

My life will have meaning after all.

The men suggested I think over their proposition and they gave me a contract to sign. They said no one would know I was working for the CIA and they told me not to tell anyone about it. A week later, I received a phone call from my father in New York.

"Are you working for the CIA?"

When I asked my father how he found out, he said two men were ringing doorbells in our building, asking questions about me, and telling everyone they were with the CIA.

This was definitely the most exciting thing that ever happened to me. It was as if everything I had done was in preparation for this moment. Learning German at the Ethical Culture Fieldston School and the coincidence that I had no trace of an American accent were two of many fortuitous events that had paved the way for my career as a spy.

Linda and I agreed that before I officially started working for the CIA, we would telephone her parents and tell them what I was about to do. Although this was a violation of my agreement, it seemed prudent because we were living in an isolated city, sur-rounded by Russian-dominated East Germany. The excitement of telling my father about my new occupation had outweighed any concern that my cover had been blown before even starting the job. When I telephoned Tom Cabot, he said he was worried Linda might be kidnapped and held for ransom if I was discovered.

Two weeks after our first meeting, I waited at the Maison de France, as arranged, for the CIA agents to reappear. In my pocket was the signed contract with the United States government for the unknown feats I was about to perform, along with a clause that included my promise not to disclose anything about my mission for 18 years. As a child, I had often been attracted to danger. When my mother told me not to put my hand on the hot radiator, I touched it immediately to see if I could get away with not getting burned. I also jumped off the end of my bed in an attempt to fly, and once I ran back and forth across the street in between the cars, which resulted in my father tying me to my bed. Now, in Berlin, I was about to court danger for a different reason. As long as I remained married to Linda, I was safe from the pitfalls of the everyday working man, but this was not enough. My conscience gnawed at the safety net that held me. I would only be working part-time for the CIA, but maybe if I did a good job I could become a full-time employee.

Instead of the agents, a different man sat down at my table. He told me his name was George Connors, and he said he would be my contact at the agency. After I handed him my signed contract, he gave me his telephone number.

* * *

Through Herman Weissenborn I learned of a young harpsichordist who had just arrived in Berlin from East Germany. He was interested in the love songs I had been performing on the radio and Weissenborn suggested I arrange a recital with him. The nature of the material, plus the fact that I was an American tenor in Berlin, was enough to convince the Amerika Haus to sponsor the event in their concert hall on Nollendorfplatz. When I wrote the news of my recital to Mori in Rome, she replied that she would arrange for me to repeat the recital in the concert hall of the Castel Sant'Angelo. Now, all of a sudden, I was about to give two concerts in Europe. Perhaps I could become the American Fischer-Dieskau.

Just before the concert in Berlin, I received word that Grandma Goldmark was dying, so I flew to New York. As she lay helplessly in her hospital bed, she seemed smaller than I had remembered. When I told her about my upcoming concerts she said, "You must be walking on air." A few days later she died. During the week I was in New York, Grandma Black also died. That left my grandfather. I would have to be worthy of his belief in me.

My Berlin concert was well-received. The morning after my recital in Rome, Mori showed me a copy of the *Paese Della Sera*, one of Rome's most important newspapers. There was an ecstatic review of my concert.

"I can't believe it!" I said. "I didn't know a critic was there!"

"He wasn't," said Mori. "I wrote it myself."

* * *

I had been living in Europe for five years. I had become a large tenor and I had learned ten operatic roles. Because I spoke Italian and German, I had made my debut in Rome and Berlin. It was time to return to America and take the operatic world by storm!

Linda and I decided to take Brigitte with us. Other famous couples returned from Africa with a caged animal. We were bringing home a German opera singer to keep me in shape for my career.

Two weeks after our return, I auditioned for opera impresario Boris Goldovsky at the Met. After my first aria, Goldovsky motioned for me to come down from the stage.

He's heard enough! He's heard enough! He's going to put me in the Met!

"Mr. Blek," said Goldovsky, "haff you zoht of trying zomzing else?"

From Socks to Stocks

I was stunned. The idea that I had wasted five years of my life and that my lifelong dream had just gone up in smoke was too frightening to contemplate. But then I realized Goldovsky didn't actually say I couldn't sing. Maybe he saw something else I could do. It turned out I wasn't far from wrong. Goldovsky had his own opera company. He told me if I paid him "a participation fee," I could be in it. I was one of four tenors. We each paid $450 to sing one act of *La Boheme* in an open-air theater in Wheeling, West Virginia, for 2,000 coal miners. I got the second act where Rodolfo has only one line to sing. I rehearsed with the orchestra and when it came time to sing my line in the performance, I was excited. Everyone was looking at me. I opened my mouth to sing and a fly flew in.

I was not ready to give up my operatic career. I had seen an ad in the *New York Times* about a voice teacher named Samuel Margolis. The headline read "Samuel Margolis is the only teacher of Robert Merrill and he can get you into the Met!" I made an appointment with Margolis who had a large studio in Carnegie Hall. There were no rugs on the floor so my voice sounded bigger. Margolis played each note he wanted me to sing loudly on the piano. His own voice was so hoarse he could hardly talk. At the end of our first session, Margolis told me he charged $100 an hour for lessons, which included a seat in his box at the Met every other month. That's what the ad meant when it said "Margolis can get you into the Met!" I thought of all the people I might meet if Margolis was my voice teacher and I was hooked.

At this point, Linda and I were living in the Cabot home in Weston, Massachusetts, the scene of our engagement party. Brigitte was giving us voice lessons in the living room. I sang as loud as I could, in case Tom or Virginia Cabot were listening.

In addition to not having a home of our own, Linda and I were trying to handle the deficiencies in our marriage. When we were students at Harvard, we used each other to clobber our fathers. Once we were married, we had achieved our purpose. During our fairy tale years in Rome and Berlin, we were surrounded by enticing distractions and never created a home for ourselves. Now, we were back in full sight of our fathers. We were still living off of Linda's money and I had no prospects for a job. Neither Linda nor I wanted to admit defeat so we decided that having children would justify our marriage.

It was time for us to think about moving out of the Cabots' living room and into a home of our own. Linda was pregnant and Brigitte was having an affair with the Cabots' family doctor. Linda had grown up with country estates, chalets in Vermont, islands in Maine, and a large family ranch in Colorado. She wanted to bring our children up in the country with horses. I knew I could never become a Cabot, but maybe I could start behaving like one.

Linda and I found an estate in Wilton, Connecticut, less than an hour away from New York. It was perched on a hill with a swimming pool and views of open country sloping down to a reservoir surrounded by riding and walking trails. There were barns with horse stalls and corrals, yellow and white cottages, and a large main house with several fireplaces. One of our neighbors was Dave Brubeck and the other was Jack Jessup, the editor of *Life* magazine.

* * *

I was about to sing with the Chautauqua Opera Company in upstate New York when I received a letter and a kit full of samples from the president of The Wilknit Hosiery Company, offering me the chance to sell socks and stockings on commission. Opera singers come in all sizes, so I took the samples with me for the weekend, and sold out my allotment. Then, I received a congratulatory letter from the president of The Wilknit Hosiery Company with a new supply of socks.

"It's demeaning for the son of Algernon Black to be selling socks," said my father's secretary. She introduced me to a friend of hers at First Investors Corporation where they sold mutual funds, so I went from socks to stocks.

Mutual funds were a way for people who had little or no money to invest in the stock market. If you had money, you could buy a selection of stocks and not put all your eggs in one basket. You could also hire a professional to choose the stocks and manage your money. Diversification and professional management were the key to successful investing in the stock market. If you only had a small amount of money to invest, you could combine it with other small investors and create a mutual fund. Then you could enjoy the same success as wealthy investors. If you had no extra money to invest, First Investors would withdraw an agreed-upon amount from your checking account every month for ten years in what was called "a contractual plan." A salesman for First Investors Corporation got one-half of his total commission for the ten years of the contractual plan in the first year, to create an incentive for the customer to stay in the plan.

I began by ringing doorbells in Harlem and selling $10-a-month plans. Then I moved to West End Avenue where I sold $100-a-month plans. One of my prospects couldn't make up his mind. Then I told him I would receive half of my commission for the whole ten years in the first year of the plan. "Let's do it," he told me. My honesty in sharing this news had helped me close the sale.

Harry Wechsler was my parent's family doctor and while he was giving me my annual exam I gave him my mutual fund pitch. Dr. Wechsler told me he would like to invest $1,200.

"You mean you would like to buy $1,200 worth of mutual funds?"

"No," said Dr. Wechsler, "I want a $1,200-a-month contractual plan for ten years."

In addition to being a doctor, Harry Wechsler was also the owner of Wechsler Coffee. His ten-year contractual plan amounted to an investment of $144,000 and was the largest contractual plan ever sold to an individual in the history of mutual funds. It also made me Salesman of the Year at First Investors Corporation.

The company held a dinner in the Grand Ballroom of the Waldorf Astoria. They presented me with a gold-plated cup with a statue of a man holding a briefcase on top, and my name was engraved underneath. I was proud of my award and I showed it to my parents.

"It doesn't look like you," said my mother.

"Capitalism doesn't work," said my father. "You're 27 years old. Why don't you find something to do that will benefit humanity?"

I went to a therapist.

"Say the first thing that comes into your mind."

"How much do you charge?"

"I am the cheapest therapist in town."

"My father is a minister who doesn't believe in God, my mother laughs at me whenever I try to accomplish anything, and I am wasting my life on Wall Street."

"Could you recommend some good stocks?" asked the therapist.

Although I did not have my parents' approval, it seemed to me I was in good shape. I had the most expensive voice teacher and the cheapest therapist in town.

My success with Dr. Wechsler started me thinking. If the purpose of mutual funds was to help investors keep pace with inflation, what about the millions of people who received their pensions through unions? When they became eligible for their pensions, the plans would be worth less than the money they invested. I was in my second year as the top salesman at First Investors Corporation and the mutual-fund industry was enjoying popularity through the likes of Bernie Cornfeld and others. Wall Street brokerage houses were looking for successful mutual-fund salesmen and I was contacted by Loeb Rhoades and Burnham and Company, each of whom offered me bigger commissions if I would work for them. There were 220 different mutual funds and I noticed that one of the smallest with assets of only $20 million had the best record. It had outperformed all the common-stock funds, even though it was investing in safer triple A bonds. It was called the Guardian Fund and I went to see the managing director, Roy Neuberger.

I told Roy I thought I could get the labor unions to be his clients. I suggested he pay me a salary since Guardian was a no-load fund with no commission. I also told Roy that, if I was successful, I would like to become a partner in his firm. This would give me an incentive to increase the size of the Guardian Fund, since I would own a percentage of the firm that managed it. Roy agreed to all of my suggestions.

I left First Investors Corporation and began talking about the Guardian Fund to representatives of the International Ladies'

Garment Workers' Union and the National Maritime Union's Officers' Pension Fund. There was interest everywhere, but in each case I was told no union would invest in anything without the approval of their financial adviser, Martin E. Segal.

I took the second vice-president of Martin E. Segal's company out to lunch, and worked my way up the corporate ladder. Eventually, I met Martin E. Segal, who was small physically but powerful financially. He was the adviser and actuary for $15 billion of union and pension funds. Over lunch, I told Segal how mutual funds could help keep pace with inflation for his union's pension trusts and about the investment record of the Guardian Fund, which had outperformed the common-stock funds even during the Depression years when they were more conservatively invested. When I told him there would be no sales charge, Segal's eyes brightened considerably. "I will be your first customer with $45,000 from my own company," said Segal. "Then, I will give you letters of recommendation about Guardian for all the unions and companies that are paying me for advice."

As I danced away from our meeting, I had a sense of unreality. Was it a dream? Would Martin Segal change his mind before the $45,000 check cleared? It was the same anxiety that would haunt me all through my life whenever I achieved anything. My father would not approve and my mother would laugh at me.

Martin Segal did not change his mind. Along with his check came copies of letters he wrote introducing me to some of his clients, including the International Ladies' Garment Workers' Union, the National Maritime Union's Officers' Pension Fund, and the Research Foundation for the State University of New York, which was supported by federal funds. This meant the United States Government was now one of my clients.

When I told my therapist about my new clients, she said she would like to buy some shares in the Guardian Fund. This presented a problem. I was looking for her advice, not her money. If she lost money, would she still be able to help me? I wasn't sure she was helping me anyway. When I entered her living room for my therapy session, holding a newspaper, she wanted to see the headlines. Sometimes, she read a whole article while I waited. During our sessions, my therapist answered the telephone, and ate food that she brought in from her kitchen. She drank tea and smoked cigarettes. I found this distracting. When I told her I was frustrated because she wasn't saying anything, she puffed on her cigarette and smiled.

The hall of my therapist's apartment served as her waiting room. While I was waiting, I could hear the patient ahead of me talking through the living room door that served as her "office." That meant everyone else could hear me as well. The only advantage to hearing the previous patient was that I learned I was not the only one delivering long monologues to the therapist without getting any response. The patient ahead of me was sad and depressed when he left, and he avoided looking at me because he knew I had heard everything he said.

"Why Don't You Become a Broadway Producer?"

After several months of acquiring labor unions as clients, I was feeling strangely dissatisfied. The excitement of selling had disappeared. All I had to do was tell a union official that Martin E. Segal was my client and I would have another customer.

One evening in the summer of 1959, I went to a party at the Dakota on Central Park West.

"Why do you look so unhappy?" asked a former Harvard classmate. "You're making money!"

"I'm making money on Wall Street but I always wanted to be in show business."

"Why don't you become a Broadway producer?"

"What does a Broadway producer do?"

"He finds a play, hires a star and a director, raises the money, and becomes rich and famous."

"When can I start?"

"Right now," said my friend. "I'm an agent and I have a show for you."

I can't believe it! My grandfather's living room where I produced "The Greatest Show off Earth!" is on the next block. Now, it's really happening!

The musical that was to make me rich and famous was *Flora Pasquale Strikes Back!* — the story of actress Evita Peron. When Evita married the president of Argentina, she had the drama critic who criticized her performances banished from the country. This was the subject of the musical. The budget for the off-Broadway production of *Flora Pasquale Strikes Back!* was $45,000. I was in such a hurry to become rich and famous that I raised all the money without reading the script. After I read it, I gave the investors their money back. A well-known producer named Saint Subber heard that someone gave money back to investors. He wanted to meet me. Subber needed $40,000 to complete the $100,000 budget for a new play called *Look, We've Come Through!* about six young people who were trying to survive in New York City. It was written by Hugh Wheeler and was to be directed by the award-winning director Jose Quintero, who had directed the original Broadway production of Eugene O'Neill's *Long Day's Journey into Night.* There were six unknown actors in the cast and they were each being paid $125 a week. One of them was Burt Reynolds. This time, I read the script and I liked it.

Subber told me if I could raise the $40,000 in six weeks I would have my name next to his as the co-producer and a share of the profits. I bought Leo Shull's book, *Angels,* for $6.75, which listed all the people who had recently invested in Broadway shows. I remembered my experience selling mutual funds, when I told my first prospect that half of my commission would be deducted in the first year. It had resulted in my first sale. I told prospective investors the odds of investing in a hit Broadway show were four to one against it, but I also explained that if the show was a hit they would not only receive money from the Broadway production, but from amateur, motion picture, and stock rights as well for a period of 18 years. I raised $25,000 from people in the *Angels* book and I was $15,000 short with three days left. Miraculously, I was invited to a second party at the Dakota. This time, the host was Warner LeRoy, the owner of Maxwell's Plum, and there were many guests from the world of entertainment.

"Hello, I'm David Black and if I can raise $15,000 by Saturday, I'll be a Broadway producer!" —- "Hello, I'm David Black and if I can raise $15,000 by Saturday, I'll be a Broadway producer!"

"Come with me," said a young man. He took me down to a pier on the West Side where the *Andrea Doria* had just docked. She hadn't sunk yet. We met a disembarking passenger named William Ball of the Ball Mason Jars Corporation of Muncie, Indiana. I talked to Mr. Ball for an hour in his hotel room, and he wrote me a check for $15,000.

* * *

"I'm going to be a Broadway producer!"

"You want to produce Broadway shows so you can fill theaters that have more seats than your father's church," said my therapist. "I would like tickets for opening night."

On opening night of *Look, We've Come Through!* I was excited.

My parents are coming! The critics are coming! My name will be in the papers!

The theater was full. I was nervous. What if one of the actors got sick or forgot his lines? The critic for the *New York Times* was late. The moment he arrived, the curtain went up.

When the curtain came down at the end of the play, I got a chill up and down my spine during the applause and bravos. The opening night party took place at Sardi's. The investors were hoping they had bet on the right show. I was about to become rich and famous! At midnight, the press agent arrived with a stack of newspapers. Everyone began reading the reviews. They looked good to me.

"They're not good enough," said Saint Subber, shaking his head. "We don't have a star so we needed rave reviews."

Look, We've Come Through! did not come through. No one had ever heard of Burt Reynolds.

At this point, Linda and I were basking in a success of our own. Her name was Sophie and she was gorgeous and cute, and we didn't need critics to tell us she was a smash hit. Sophie was trying to stand up and get to know the world. Although she didn't know it, Sophie had arrived when I needed her. As a Broadway producer, I would have to have a hit show. If I failed and had to give up, Sophie would be there to comfort me.

* * *

One week after the closing of *Look, We've Come Through!* I received a phone call from the secretary for Sol Hurok, who told me Mr. Hurok was inviting me to lunch. Sol Hurok had become a world-famous impresario when he arranged for Russia's Bolshoi Ballet to perform in New York during the Cuban Missile Crisis. As a result, Hurok had 4,000 clients. I had come across Hurok's name in the *Angels* book and had made my pitch to one of his vice presidents. Hurok, whom I never met, had invested $15,000 in *Look, We've Come Through!*

Broadway shows are usually financed by limited partnerships. The producer is the general partner and the investors are limited partners. The investors supply the financing and any money earned by the show goes toward paying them back first. After the investors have recouped their money, they split the profits 50/50 with the producer. A Broadway producer does not risk any of his own money but he cannot make any profits until the investors have recouped their total investment. A producer also receives a weekly fee from the box office receipts for the expenses of keeping his office running. When Saint Subber closed *Look, We've Come Through!* only two-thirds of the $100,000 producing costs had been spent. Most producers would have kept the show running so they could help themselves to their weekly fee but Saint Subber was more concerned with his reputation than the money. He closed the show after four performances and refunded the remaining one-third of the money to the investors.

"Mr. Black," said Sol Hurok during a sumptuous lunch at Le Cirque. "I have been in this business for 110 years and I never got money back on a flop. From now on, I will invest in everything you produce."

* * *

When I co-produced *Look, We've Come Through!* I met Audrey Wood, who represented the playwright Hugh Wheeler. Audrey was the best-known talent agent on Broadway and Tennessee Williams was her most famous client. She had just made headlines for dumping a plate of salad on Tennessee's head when he said something off-color during their lunch at Sardi's. Audrey attended some of our rehearsals for *Look, We've Come Through!* and she told me she thought I could have a successful producing career. She offered me an exciting new play for my first solo production. It was called *The Aspern Papers*.

The Aspern Papers was an adaptation of a Henry James novel by the English actor Sir Michael Redgrave, about a man who goes to Venice to search for the lost poems of a dead poet. The play had been a hit in London with Redgrave himself in the lead. I assembled an international cast for Broadway: star of stage and screen Dame Wendy Hiller from London; Francoise Rosay, star of the Comedie-Francaise in Paris; and as the maid, an unknown American actress named Olympia Dukakis. For the lead, I chose Ralph Bellamy, who had just appeared as Franklin Roosevelt in the film *Sunrise at Campobello*, and to direct, I signed England's most prominent director, Dame Margaret Webster.

When I went to the airport to pick up Dame Margaret, I was excited. I expected her to speak in iambic pentameter in keeping with her status as Britain's number-one Shakespearean director. In the limousine, she told me she had written a poem. Her agent was Peter Watt, and she knew that my agent was Peter Witt. "Peter Watt is a bit of a clot," said Dame Margaret, "but not such a shit as Peter Witt."

In real life, Ralph Bellamy was the president of Actor's Equity, the union representing all the actors in America. While we were negotiating his contract for *The Aspern Papers*, Bellamy was in Washington testifying before Congress about the terrible state of American theater. When I got back to my office after picking up Dame Margaret, Bellamy called me. He said he was happy with the financial terms of his contract but he wanted a limousine to take him to the theater every night. When I said I couldn't afford it, Bellamy said, "Oh, that's all right. I won't use it, but leave it in the contract so I can tell the next producer I got it from you." I could not believe that the president of the actor's union, who had just played Franklin Roosevelt on the screen, could make such a suggestion. I told Bellamy I couldn't do what he wanted and we parted company. I was two weeks' away from rehearsals with no leading man. Then I heard that Maurice Evans was available.

Maurice Evans was known for his Hamlet and for his recording of *Winnie-the-Pooh*. Unfortunately for *The Aspern Papers*, Maurice Evans turned out to be more Winnie-the-Pooh than Hamlet. Maurice had never met Michael Redgrave, so he and his partner invited Michael Redgrave and his partner to dinner in their town house. Maurice told me he wanted to suggest a few revisions in the script and I advised him to be diplomatic with Michael. I suggested he wait until after dinner to discuss what he wanted. Early in the evening, I received a phone call from a very angry Michael Redgrave. He told me there was a copy of his script under the grapefruit appetizer. Pages and scenes had been crossed out in red and replaced with new dialogue written by Maurice. Michael and his partner had walked out of Maurice's dinner.

I remembered a course I took at Harvard, which said theater was "heightened reality." If this was true, the reality of the people I was working with was heightened in the wrong direction. Were they that way when they first got into theater, or was theater responsible for their condition? Either way, I would have to deal with them.

I remembered my father smoked a pipe when he wasn't talking. It gave him something to hold on to and it created an impression of authority even when he wasn't smoking it. At the next rehearsal, I not only smoked a pipe but I blew the smoke between Michael and Maurice.

At the first matinee of *The Aspern Papers* in New Haven, after Michael Redgrave had gone back to New York, Maurice recited a speech he had written, which turned his character from a villain into a hero.

"If that speech stays in," said Wendy Hiller, "I'm on the next plane to London."

"If I can't do my speech, I'm leaving the show," said Maurice.

I phoned Michael and we agreed it would not be a bad thing if Maurice *did* leave the show, because then Michael could take over the role he had already successfully played in London. At the next performance, Maurice Evans spotted Michael Redgrave sitting in the audience and the speech suddenly disappeared.

Then, Wendy Hiller complained to me that Maurice was refusing to kiss her in the love scenes. She wanted the lights turned down so no one could see what was not happening. By the time we got to Philadelphia, the love scenes were being played in almost total darkness.

In Philadelphia, the actress playing a featured role in the play told me her aunt was sick. She wanted to visit her in New York because they had a close relationship, and she assured me she would only miss the matinee, and would return for the evening performance. The actress never came back. A few days later, her agent called and told me she had auditioned for the film *To Kill a Mockingbird* opposite Gregory Peck, and got the part. She was leaving the show. This left us without an important member of the cast with only ten days left before opening on Broadway. Maurice and I went to see another play in Philadelphia and found a replacement.

I told my therapist that producing was making me nervous.

"Why don't you join me at the opera?" she suggested. "I have an extra ticket."

I was trying to forget about opera, but I wanted my therapist to like me so I agreed to join her. Then, she thumbed through the pages of a large book she kept on a shelf. "Aha!" she said, excitedly writing out a prescription. "Take some of these pills whenever you feel nervous." I took several of the pills before picking her up for our date at the opera.

The Aspern Papers received rave reviews: "*The Aspern Papers* is a literary masterpiece," said the *New York Times*. "It is as rare as it is rewarding!" "*The Aspern Papers* is one of the most exciting plays of the season!" said the *Daily News*. The play ran for a year and won awards, but the theater was never full and the show did not recover its cost of $125,000. Not enough people were interested in the lost poems of a dead poet.

A Harvard classmate of mine named Jerome Kilty gave me a play he had written based on Thornton Wilder's great novel, *The Ides of March,* about the last days of the Roman Empire. I sent the script to Sir John Gielgud in London, inviting him to play Julius Caesar, and I received a letter back from Gielgud saying, "Dear Mr. Black, This is a beautifully written play but I don't feel I am capable of playing the part."

I jumped on a plane to London and went to see Gielgud in a play at the Haymarket Theatre. After the performance, I went backstage and introduced myself. "I wouldn't be here if you didn't like the script," I told Sir John. "But who else could play the part?"

I took Sir John to Berlin to see a performance of *The Ides of March* in German. Gielgud did not understand a word of German. I hired a group of people I knew from the Berlin opera houses who were paid to applaud at key moments. Whenever the actor playing Julius Caesar made an entrance, he got a round of applause and at the end he received a standing ovation. Gielgud agreed to play the part.

In England, great actors are knighted by the Queen. Gielgud had been knighted and shared that honor with Sir Laurence Olivier and Sir Michael Redgrave. One of Gielgud's conditions for accepting my offer to star in *The Ides of March* was that he would also be the director. Some Hollywood stars direct themselves in movies but in the theater there is no way for an actor to observe himself and the rest of the cast at the same time. Attempting it could be a recipe for disaster. Without Gielgud, I would not be able to raise the money to produce the show. I would have to take a chance and let Gielgud direct.

As director, Gielgud had the final word on casting. One day, he invited me to lunch to meet his choice for the actress he wanted to play his wife, Calpurnia, second only in beauty to Cleopatra. When I walked into the restaurant, Gielgud was sitting with a woman who looked old enough to be his mother, and she was dressed like a bag lady. During lunch I was polite, but horrified. At the end of our meal, Gielgud suggested we go to the Haymarket Theatre where they would read a scene for me.

There was only a work light and Gielgud and the actress walked up on the stage and opened their scripts in semi-darkness. While Gielgud was reading his lines, the actress was listening and when she started to speak she became the second most beautiful woman in the world. Her name was Irene Worth.

The Ides of March opened to critical acclaim in London, but Gielgud did not want to take a chance with it on Broadway.

* * *

One morning, three gentlemen walked into my New York office. They were well dressed and looked proud of themselves. They told me their names were Meyers, Schwartz, and Harrow, and they said they had just sold 37 Wall Street for $40 million. They were looking for promising young people to invest in and they had been watching me and thought I would make a successful Broadway producer. They proposed creating a company called David Black Associates, which would receive all the profits from my shows. We would each own 25 percent of the company and I would never have to raise money again. In addition to providing the financing for my shows, Meyers, Schwartz, and Harrow promised me unlimited "front money" to acquire new plays and musicals. They would also pay me a salary to work for myself and rent a larger office for David Black Associates.

To accept the Meyers, Schwartz, and Harrow deal, I would be giving up three-quarters of my income for the rest of my life but the offer of unlimited financing was too good to turn down. Most of my time was spent raising money on each new production. If I was free of that responsibility, I could probably produce more shows and increase the odds of having a hit. I deliberated for a few minutes and then I said yes. The gentlemen found new office space for me next to the Museum of Modern Art and they arranged two parties to celebrate our partnership.

Musicals were more successful than plays on Broadway and I had never produced one. They were hard to come by because most successful composers usually return to the producers with whom they had success. One day, as I searched for a possible subject for a musical, I found myself thinking of Sally Bowles in Christopher Isherwood's *The Berlin Stories*. Sally is a girl from London who's having a knockabout career as a nightclub singer in the early days of Hitler's Berlin. I had read the story at Harvard and I was reminded of it when I lived in Berlin. There was the same feeling of decadence when I lived there in the 1950s as there had been when Hitler first came to power. There were bicycle races in the Sportpalast, dueling societies, and very racy nightclubs. It seemed to me that Isherwood's Sally Bowles would make a great leading lady for a Broadway musical, so I found his number in the phone book and invited him for dinner at the Chelsea Hotel. I didn't realize the significance of my choice of venue until we were having our first drink. Sally Bowles was a native of Chelsea in London! Isherwood was excited about my idea and during a second round of drinks I wrote him a check for $500, for which I acquired the right to make a Broadway musical out of *The Berlin Stories*.

When I was producing *The Ides of March* in London, Sir John Gielgud had introduced me to Julie Andrews. After acquiring the rights to *The Berlin Stories* from Isherwood, I invited Julie to play Sally Bowles. Julie loved the idea and she introduced me to Sandy Wilson who had written *The Boy Friend*, the show that had made her a star. Sandy wrote eight new songs and we called the new musical *Goodbye to Berlin.*

When I was leaving London, Julie was about to give birth to her first child and she was also getting divorced from her husband, the English set designer, Tony Walton. I visited Julie in the hospital and admired her new baby girl. Julie told me about a new English play called *Semi-Detached*, which concerned the adventures of a salesman in British suburbia. It was written by David Turner, the creator of the immensely successful BBC radio soap-opera, *The Archers. Semi-Detached* was going to open in London's West End starring none other than Sir Laurence Olivier, the third member of the Queen's holy trinity of knighted actors! Julie offered to get me a copy of the script. She told me if I liked it she would introduce me to the English producer Oscar Lewenstein so I could get the rights to produce the play on Broadway with Laurence Olivier. I read the script with excitement on the plane back to New York. My new partners Meyers, Schwartz, and Harrow thought it would be a great coup if I could produce *Semi-Detached* on Broadway starring the world's greatest actor, Laurence Olivier. However, Oscar Lewenstein, the English producer, had co-produced many successful shows with David Merrick, the king of all Broadway producers. I had to make sure Merrick wasn't interested.

"David, my boy," said David Merrick over lunch at Sardi's, "you are just what the theater needs! New young producing talent! I wouldn't think of standing in your way! Besides, I have three shows running, including *Hello, Dolly!* and I'm on the cover of *Time* magazine this week. Go get the play and have a big success with it!"

I flew to London, missing the parties for my new office, and offered Oscar Lewenstein the standard $500 for the American rights. Lewenstein excused himself. He came back a few minutes later and told me he had just spoken to David Merrick in New York and Merrick had offered him $600. I couldn't believe Merrick would do such a thing. I raised my offer to $700. Merrick said $800. I was locked in a battle with the world's most famous producer over which of us would get the rights to present the world's most famous actor. When I was forced to bid $10,000, I begged Oscar Lewenstein not to call Merrick. When he left to make the call, I burst into tears.

An hour later, I became the owner of the American rights to *Semi- Detached* for the sum of $25,000. The *New York Times* ran a headline that announced, "New Producer Beats David Merrick." The story reported that $25,000 was the highest sum ever paid for an option on a play in the history of the American theater.

I had never met Laurence Olivier and I went to see him in *Uncle Vanya* at the Chichester Festival Theatre, where he was both star and director. Afterwards, I told him how moved I was by his performance.

"Did you really think I was any good?" asked Olivier.

My father had asked me the same question when I first heard him speak. Did Olivier really want to know what I thought, or was he acting? Olivier had a reputation for taking risks. On opening night of *Semi-Detached* in London, he adopted a very thick Midlands accent. No one could understand a word he said. The play was a flop. My partners lost $25,000, and David Merrick was still the king of Broadway.

"I dreamed I was riding on the carousel in Central Park," I told my therapist. "My horse turned into a lion and started chasing me! I ran out of Central Park to escape from the lion and into the Ethical Culture Society. David Merrick was sitting in my father's chair waiting to give the Sunday talk!"

"Double the dose of the nervous pills," said my therapist.

My new partners were not happy about losing money and they suggested I find a way to recoup it. If they stayed with me they would be losing a lot more than $25,000, but since this was our first venture together, I came up with a plan to recoup their loss. Laurence Olivier had originally seen *Semi-Detached* at the well-known Belgrade Theatre in Coventry, England, where it was a great success. A popular actor and television star, Leonard Rossiter, had played the lead. I decided to bring the original Coventry company, including Rossiter, to Broadway. In return, I promised Actor's Equity I would export an American acting company with an equal number of American actors to London in a play of their choice. This added another $25,000 to the budget for the Broadway production of *Semi-Detached*, which was paid by the investors and went into the pockets of Meyers, Schwartz, and Harrow.

I was able to get the Music Box Theater, one of Broadway's best theaters, for *Semi-Detached* and Leonard Rossiter was hilarious in the previews. Rossiter was not a name so we would have to "paper" the house to make sure it was packed for opening night. Whatever the critics thought of the play, they would not be able to ignore an audience roaring with laughter.

Several days before the opening night of *Semi-Detached*, I asked our company manager how the tickets were selling. He told me they were going really well and not to worry about papering the house because it would be sold out. On opening night, I was horrified to see the theater was less than half full with only a smattering of critics and investors. If the company manager had been honest with me, we could have filled the house, drawing from lists of organizations that love to get free tickets. My company manager had "The Greek Messenger's Syndrome," the fear of delivering bad news. I fired him but it was too late. Critics and investors do not laugh, so the theater was filled with a deathly silence during the opening-night performance. *Semi-Detached* closed on opening night.

* * *

Because of the story in the *New York Times* about how I out-bid David Merrick for *Semi-Detached*, I found myself in demand as a Broadway producer. My doorman handed me a play written by his mother. My grandfather's male nurse reached under the blanket covering my grandfather in his wheelchair and handed me an original script. Plays were piling up in my office. One of them was *Ready When You Are, C.B.!* about an actress who threw up at auditions and rented out her apartment to movie stars. The playwright was a former casting director named Susan Slade who had worked as a secretary for Marlon Brando and had an imaginary love affair with him. I sent the script to Julie Harris, the only actress to ever win five Tony awards, and Julie agreed to play the lead. Then I hired the Pulitzer Prize-winning coauthor and director of *South Pacific*, Joshua Logan, to direct.

When we were holding auditions for the important role of Julie's best friend in the play, an actress gave a reading that was so funny that Julie, Josh, and I all burst into laughter simultaneously. I signed the actress to a run-of-the-play contract and she was never funny again. She wasn't funny in rehearsals. She wasn't funny in previews. She wasn't funny on stage or off! How could this happen? I was a new producer but Julie Harris and Joshua Logan were already legends in the theater! How could veteran talent make such a mistake? And more to the point, why could the actress never achieve the level of performance she had displayed in her audition?

The more shows I produced, the more mystified I became about the creative process in theater. Each new show seemed to have more problems than the last. When we were trying out *Ready When You Are, C.B.!* in Philadelphia, I was awakened at three in the morning by a knock on the door of my hotel room. When I looked through the peephole, it was Joshua Logan in a white terry-cloth bathrobe holding a tray of sandwiches.

"We are in trouble," said Josh. "Making Julie unhappy is like throwing a rock through a Rembrandt. The audience loves Julie and if the leading man leaves her at the end the play, it will be a flop." Josh told me it would be easy to come up with a happy ending. He said we could slide a phone booth onstage and the leading man could call Julie from the airport and say he had changed his mind and wanted to spend the rest of his life with her. When I asked Josh when he was planning to talk to playwright Susan Slade about this new ending, he said, "I am not going to do it, you are." It seemed to me this was the director's job but Josh was a bit stressed so I decided to speak to Susan myself.

When I told Susan about Josh's suggestion, she said, "But David, it didn't happen that way." I explained that theater is make-believe and that the audience had fallen in love with Julie Harris and wanted her to be happy. "But that's not *my* story!" said Susan.

New plays open out of town so they can make adjustments with live audiences before facing the New York critics. That's why they are called "out-of-town tryouts." The playwright's union, the Dramatists Guild of America, does not allow anyone to change an "and," "if," or a "but" without the playwright's permission. If the play-wright refuses to try anything new during the out-of-town tryout, a producer's only recourse is to close the play and not take it to New York. My friend, David Merrick, was famous for doing just that.

With *Ready When You Are, C.B.!* there was another problem. After I signed Julie Harris and Joshua Logan, I made a preproduction movie deal with Paramount Pictures who offered me $250,000 for the movie rights. Paramount believed that the play would be a hit and wanted to secure the movie rights ahead of the other studios. To earn the $250,000 for my investors, the play would have to run 21 performances on Broadway. If I closed the play out of town, Susan Slade would get our $250,000 in addition to her regular royalties. Susan knew this so she refused to even try Josh's happy ending.

When I told Josh I had news about my meeting with Susan, he asked me to join him at a Philadelphia Eagles football game. He said watching football would help him relax, whatever the news. When I described Susan's refusal to try the happy ending he said he had a premonition about how she would react, which was why he asked me to talk to her.

During the game, Josh told me he had been diagnosed with manic-depressive illness and had been hospitalized twice. He told me about a new drug called Lithium, which he was hoping to try.

"Without the manic phase of my illness, I would have lived only half of my life," said Josh. "I would have missed the sharpest, rarest, and the sweetest moments of my existence."

Ready When You Are, C.B.! opened in New York at the Brooks Atkinson Theater and closed after four performances. A few months later, Susan Slade committed suicide.

* * *

I had been producing Broadway shows for four years, but all the drama was happening backstage. Everyone I dealt with was having an identity crisis. Ralph Bellamy, the president of Actor's Equity, wanted a limousine in his contract, even if he didn't use it. Maurice Evans inserted a speech he had written into *The Aspern Papers* because he was afraid the audience wouldn't like *him*. Sir John

Gielgud agreed to star in *The Ides of March* when he saw another actor get a standing ovation in a foreign language he didn't understand, and Sir Laurence Olivier wanted to know if I thought he was any good. David Merrick, the most famous Broadway producer in history, told me he was not interested in *Semi-Detached* and then started bidding against me, and the legendary Joshua Logan was afraid to ask novice playwright Susan Slade for a happy ending.

Susan Slade and I were the same age, 33. Susan took her own life because she did not understand the difference between the character she had written and the character Julie Harris created on the stage. Susan was not the first playwright I met with this problem. Shortly after *Ready When You Are, C.B.!* I produced a play about the cosmetics industry called *The Natural Look*. The then-unknown stars were Gene Hackman and Jerry Orbach. On the day of our Broadway opening, the playwright locked herself in her hotel room and refused to come out. I had to send for her mother.

The hardest moment in the life of a playwright comes when he first hears live actors reading his words aloud. He realizes human beings will be inhabiting the life of the characters he created. He wishes he had written a book.

At the beginning of Tennessee Williams's play, *The Glass Menagerie*, Tom, a character in the play, speaks directly to the audience: "I have tricks in my pocket and things up my sleeve but I am the opposite of the stage magician. He gives you illusion that has the appearance of truth. I give you truth in the pleasant disguise of illusion." Tennessee Williams is saying there is magic in the actor's craft but it is performed in the service of a greater truth. When Tom plays Hamlet, he is not going to be Tom, because Tom does not speak in iambic pentameter, and he is not going to be Hamlet because Hamlet does not exist. What the audience experiences will be *Tamlet*, the combination of Tom and Hamlet. This is the magical person the audience will come to care about.

If I was to continue producing Broadway shows, I needed to learn how the actor creates his magic. I decided to start with the audition, where the actor performs his magic without the help of sets, lights, costumes, and an audience that has paid for the experience.

I put up a notice at Actor's Equity for actors to join me in practice auditions and I was inundated with volunteers. Most of them had never been in a Broadway show and were hoping I would "discover" them. At our opening seminar, I told them, "There are no schools for Broadway producers. It's a matter of jumping in and learning to swim, and you will be helping me with my swimming lessons."

I began the first seminar by asking the actors to perform a monologue. My plan was to stop each actor the moment I believed he was someone else. Then, we would figure out how he did it. Ten actors performed monologues and I didn't stop any of them because I didn't believe any of them. That evening I went to a play on Broadway. I decided to continue my research by making note of the first moment I believed each actor and why. I made an exciting discovery: the first time I believed each actor was not when he was talking, but when he was listening to another actor. No wonder I didn't believe any of the actors in my seminar. They had no one to listen to!

I had learned one of the secrets of acting. Maybe if I learned more, I might produce a hit.

My First Hit

I went to the premiere of *West Side Story*, and met Leonard Bernstein at the opening-night party. Bernstein told me that he had written a new musical with Alan Jay Lerner.

Here is the show I have been waiting for! A new musical by Leonard Bernstein and the creator of My Fair Lady.

I couldn't wait to get my hands on it.

But what about David Merrick? This time, he might not give up.

I made a bid to Bernstein's agent and I never heard from him again.

A week later, I read in *Variety* that another producer had optioned the show, not David Merrick. It turned out I was lucky. The musical, *1600 Pennsylvania Avenue*, ran for seven performances and lost $2 million.

If Leonard Bernstein and Alan Jay Lerner could not guarantee a hit, maybe there was no formula for success on Broadway. My friend, the agent for *Flora Pasquale Strikes Back!* promised I would become rich and famous but it had not happened.

Was it time to start thinking about trying something else?

I was still receiving plays because of the *New York Times* story. One day, I received a script for a play called *The Impossible Years*, which was about a psychiatrist who was an expert on teenagers but who couldn't control his own daughter. The name of the leading man pursuing the psychiatrist's daughter was Bartholomew Smuts. He lived in an apartment with a wall-to-wall mattress and a window for an ashtray. At one point, the psychiatrist says to his daughter, "This morning your mother showed me your room. I would have thrown up but you would never have noticed it."

The Impossible Years was not Shakespeare, or Eugene O'Neill, or Henry James, but there was something about it that interested me.

The rhythm of the lines reminded me of Groucho Marx. The playwrights were listed as Bob Fisher and Arthur Marx and I wondered if by any chance Arthur Marx was related to Groucho. When I called up the agent who sent me the script, he told me Arthur Marx was Groucho's son. He also told me that Arthur Marx and Bob Fisher had been Bob Hope's scriptwriters. This was exciting news. I wondered if I could get Groucho to play the lead.

I spoke to Arthur Marx at his Bel Air home in LA, and I told him I wanted to produce *The Impossible Years* on Broadway. Arthur invited me to visit him in Hollywood. He did not think Groucho would play the lead but he said there were other possibilities, including Jack Benny, George Burns, and Walther Matthau. Within 24 hours, I was happily ensconced at the Beverly Hills Hotel in Hollywood. Arthur was the number-one tennis player at the Beverly Hills Country Club and that afternoon he was playing an exhibition match with tennis great Bill Tilden.

In the evening, I had dinner with Arthur, his wife Lois, Groucho, and Arthur's daughter, Linda, whose teenage antics had inspired *The Impossible Years*. Groucho told me he would have starred in the play if he had written it, but he didn't think he would have success with anyone else's material.

I returned from Hollywood with no prospect for the lead in *The Impossible Years*. Half of the stars I spoke with had no theater background, and the other half were afraid to jeopardize their film careers by appearing on Broadway.

One of my appointments was canceled, so I went to a matinee performance of a revival of one of my favorite shows, *Guys and Dolls*, at the City Center starring Alan King as Nathan Detroit. I had seen Alan telling jokes about his wife on television and I knew he was paid $45,000 a week for his vaudeville act in the Catskills, but I didn't know he could act.

During the intermission of *Guys and Dolls*, I dashed back to my office and grabbed the script of *The Impossible Years*. Then I gave it to Alan King backstage at the end of the show. He called me the next morning and said he would play the lead on one condition, that I allow him to supply half of the financing.

It turned out that Alan had a business partner named Walter Hyman, who was the owner of Maxwell Industries. Walter had a private chauffer and car, which, he informed me, were his "only extravagances." After each performance of *Guys and Dolls*, Walter and his chauffer would take Alan and me to the Improv, where Walter knew the owner. On one occasion, the dishwasher burst onto the stage and started a monologue. "Not now Dustin!" said the owner.

After Alan King signed his contract, I decided to make another preproduction movie deal just as I had done for *Ready When You Are, C.B.!* I decided to go to MGM, and I invited my co-producer, Walter Hyman, to join me on my trip to Hollywood. Walter was afraid of flying, but he told me he was so excited, he was sure he would overcome his problem. We boarded our plane at Idlewild Airport. I was sitting next to Walter and as we approached the runway for takeoff, he became visibly disturbed and started to shake. Then, he pressed the button for an attendant and began shouting that he needed to speak to the captain. The co-captain came out and Walter persuaded him to turn the plane around and go back to the terminal so he could get off.

When I arrived in Los Angeles, Walter called me. He had hailed a taxi at Idlewild Airport and told the driver to take him to California. The taxi took him to Chicago where Walter commandeered a truck, which deposited him in front of the Beverly Hills

Hotel in Hollywood just in time for our meeting with MGM. I made the movie deal and we took the train back to New York together. Our only stop was Las Vegas, where we were given deluxe treatment in return for several days of Walter's extravagant gambling.

The Impossible Years received rave reviews and ran for two-and-a-half years on Broadway and another year in London. It recouped its $140,000 investment in five weeks and made a $3 million profit in the first year of its Broadway run. In addition, the play earned royalties from amateur and stock productions for 18 years. The movie starred David Niven and earned an additional profit of $6 million.

I had produced my first hit! But how did I do it? It was an accident that my appointment was canceled, and it was an accident that I had seen Alan King in *Guys and Dolls.*

I need to have more accidents!

* * *

In the summer of 1966, I was invited by George White to produce a play for the National Playwrights Conference at the Eugene O'Neill Theater Center in Waterford, Connecticut. Others in attendance included Edward Albee, John Guare, Audrey Wood, Jose Quintero, Franchot Tone, A.R. Gurney, and Michael Stewart, who had written the book for David Merrick's biggest hit, *Hello, Dolly!* Stewart had just written a new musical called *George M!* inspired by the life and the music of George M. Cohan. He told me he had also written a play called *Those That Play the Clowns*, based on Hamlet's play within the play, and he said if I produced his play, he would let me produce *George M!* He had made the same offer to David Merrick, who had turned him down, calling it blackmail. Here was my chance to get even with David Merrick! I produced *Those That*

Play the Clowns with Alfred Drake and Joan Greenwood and it was an immediate flop. Then, I turned my attention to *George M!*

* * *

Most playwrights balk at writing the book for a musical because they know whenever there is an important scene it will end up as a song. Michael Stewart had given up writing plays, except for *Those That Play the Clowns*, and he had become a highly successful book writer for Broadway musicals. His hit shows included *Bye Bye Birdie, Carnival, Barnum, 42nd Street*, and *Hello, Dolly!*

George M! was a musical retelling of the life of George M. Cohan, the only man in the history of the theater to write the book, music, and lyrics for his shows and also produce, direct, and star in them at the same time. The show was based on the film *Yankee Doodle Dandy*, which had starred the tough-talking, tap-dancing, singing dynamo James Cagney, who won the Oscar for his portrayal of Cohan in the film. I needed a theatrical James Cagney for *George M!*

I also needed a book writer like Michael Stewart to join Julie Andrews and Sandy Wilson for *Goodbye to Berlin*, and one day the producer Harold Prince called and asked me whether I would let him take over the project. Hal had two writers named John Kander and Fred Ebb who had a new concept for the show and he offered to make me his silent partner if I would let him be the producer.

Cabaret opened in 1966 on my birthday, November 20, and Hal gave me tickets in the fourth-row center for opening night. When Joel Grey made his entrance as the Emcee, singing "Wilkommen," I knew I had found my star. Joel did not have billing above the title, so at the opening night party for *Cabaret* I offered him star billing if he would play Cohan after he left *Cabaret*. Joel agreed. I also hired a new singing actress to play Cohan's sister opposite Joel. Her name was Bernadette Peters.

The budget for *George M!* was $500,000. I arranged a 45-minute musical audition at Sardi's, played and sung by Michael Stewart. Again, I told the perspective investors the odds were four to one they would lose their money. I also explained that if *George M!* was a hit the unforgettable music would result in revenues from amateur and stock productions for many years. *George M!* was financed at Sardi's in half an hour.

George M! was due to open on Broadway on April 10, 1968 at the Palace Theater, in plenty of time for the Tony Awards deadline of April 20. When we were trying out the show in Detroit, I received a phone call from the League of New York Theaters. They told me David Merrick had persuaded the League to advance the cut-off date for the Tony Awards from April 20 to April 6, thus making it impossible for *George M!* to qualify.

Before the League agreed to let Merrick change the Tony deadline date for opening on Broadway, *George M!* was the favorite to win all the Tonys. After changing the date, David Merrick's musical *Hallelujah, Baby!* would win all the Tonys because no other new musicals had opened in time for the deadline.

I had my lawyers get an injunction to prevent the Tony Awards from being televised. No producer had ever done this, and it was heavily publicized. After several days, Merrick got his lawyers to remove my injunction. I did not have the time or the money to continue the case because *George M!* was still in its out-of-town tryout in Detroit. Unlike the Oscars, a Tony is awarded in every category even if there are no nominations. When the court removed my injunction, David Merrick won all the Tony Awards for *Hallelujah, Baby!* even though it had already closed.

When *George M!* opened on Broadway, the *New York Times* theater critic Clive Barnes wrote, "It's too bad *George M!* was not allowed to compete in the Tonys, so I am giving it my personal Tony Award and Joel Grey can have two." This review by Clive Barnes turned *George M!* into an instant hit.

It was 1968, and the night before the presidential election, I wired $500 to Hubert Humphrey because I did not want to watch Richard Nixon on television for four years. Five days after the election, my secretary said, "President-elect Nixon is on the telephone!"

"What else is new?"

"Get on the phone!"

When I picked up the phone, it was Rose-Mary Woods, "Mr. Black, it's an historic moment in the history of our country when a President-elect first appears in public and President-elect Nixon has decided that his first public appearance will be at *George M!*"

My first thought was that, since Lincoln, very few presidents have gone to the theater. If Nixon actually showed up, *George M!* would run forever! Nixon wanted seven free tickets — for himself, Pat, Julie, Tricia, and three gentlemen named Haldeman, Ehrlichman, and Dean.

I was alone with Nixon in a small room backstage during intermission. He told me how he used to sit in the balcony of our theater as a kid, and about his piano lessons. Nixon was sweating and trying to impress me and he had just been elected president of the United States.

Nixon is nervous talking to me because I am a Broadway producer.

Nixon liked *George M!* and he invited me to bring it to the White House. He also asked me to produce his Inaugural Gala.

"Stay away from him!" said my father. "He's a Republican!"

"He has a very poor record in low-cost housing," said my mother.

Jack Kennedy had invited Frank Sinatra to produce his Inaugural Gala and Richard Nixon had invited me. I decided to accept.

I told Nixon if I produced his Inaugural Gala, I wanted a free hand. I was planning to invite the singer James Brown and I didn't want any Republicans walking out during his performance. Nixon said he had someone in mind who would solve all my problems. He introduced me to his lawyer, Leonard Garment, who said the budget for the Inaugural Gala was $2 million. He also told me I could hire anyone I wanted.

I produced President Nixon's Inaugural Gala in the Washington Armory on the Saturday night before the Monday inauguration. There were 10,000 people in the audience, including members of the Army, Navy, Marines, and Air Force, astronauts back from space, members of the Supreme Court, members of Congress, leaders from around the world, Vice-President-elect Spiro Agnew, and President-elect Richard Nixon.

Just before the show was about to start, I spotted some ushers giving out passes to anyone who wanted to sit in the VIP section of the audience. When I told this to Nixon, he got nervous and immediately left with his security people. Nixon and Agnew watched the gala from a nearby hotel.

The Inaugural Gala lasted nine hours and included Tony Bennett, Johnny Carson, Dinah Shore, Connie Francis, Lionel Hampton, James Brown, Doc Severinsen and the NBC Tonight Show Orchestra. For the finale, Joel Grey, Bernadette Peters, and the entire cast of *George M!* were dressed in red, white, and blue costumes, waving American flags while they sang, "You're a Grand Old Flag." Then Buddy Ebsen, TV's Jed Clampett in *The Beverly Hillbillies*, stepped forward to speak the closing words:

"I am delighted and honored to have been invited here to the inauguration," said Buddy. "And I think I'll stick around for the impeachment."

* * *

The cost of producing Broadway shows was going up and I needed to find easier ways of raising money. I promised a young man he could have billing as my co-producer for *Alice*, my new rock musical based on *Alice in Wonderland*, if he could raise $300,000, half of the $600,000 budget.

The young man introduced me to Lila Dewitt Wallace, the founder of *Reader's Digest*, which was the best-selling consumer magazine in the United States. Its global editions reached an additional 40 million people in more than 70 countries, making it the largest-paid circulation magazine in the world. During lunch at a fashionable restaurant, Mrs. Dewitt Wallace told me she would provide the whole $600,000. After she left in her chauffeured limousine, my would-be co-producer danced in the street.

When I got back to my office I received a phone call.

"Mr. Black, this is Mr. Dewitt Wallace. I understand you had lunch with my wife and she agreed to finance your show. I won't allow her to do it!"

My heart sank. "I'm sorry to hear that, Mr. Wallace. Could we meet and talk about it?"

"David, can't you take a joke?" It was my would-be co-producer.

An hour later, I received another phone call.

"Mr. Black, this is Mr. Dewitt Wallace."

"Enough is enough!"

"Mr. Black," the voice persisted, "I understand you had lunch with my wife today and she promised to back your show. She's not going to do it!" Then, he hung up.

Now, I was angry and I called my co-producer.

"That wasn't me," he said. "I only called you once."

The same young man told me he had another prospect for *Alice* who would be waiting for me at the Copacabana nightclub. It was noon and I was expecting to see "The Copacabana Girls" or Martin and Lewis rehearsing, but there was only one well-dressed gentleman sitting alone at a table.

"How much money do you need?" he asked me.

"Six-hundred thousand dollars gets us to opening night. Then, if we get good reviews, we will be on our way."

"When do you need the money?"

"As soon as we have all the financing, we can book a theater and begin casting."

"And how long do you need the money for?"

"If we get bad reviews, the money would be lost."

"I'm not worried about reviews. Just tell me how long you want the money for. You can have it for two or three years. I just need to know when I am getting it back."

"You could lose all your money if the show is a flop, but then you would get an ordinary income-tax deduction."

"I don't mind losing the money. I just need to know when I'm getting it back."

I excused myself to go to the men's room. Then I left the Copa by the back door and got lost in the crowd.

* * *

I heard a beautiful song sung by a beautiful young woman at a night club called the Village Gate. The name of the song was "Tomorrow is the First Day of the Rest of My Life." The singer told me it came from a new rock musical called *Salvation*, which was written by her boyfriend, C.C. Courtney.

Courtney told me that he had conceived of the show during a half-hour walk through Central Park while he was trying to figure out if organized religion was relevant to the needs of society. At the end of his walk, Courtney ended up in front of the Ethical Culture Society. But the plot of *Salvation* was the opposite of Ethical Culture. Courtney played a young Hard-Shell-Baptist who becomes enthralled by the pageantry and ritual of Roman Catholicism. He doesn't want to hear anyone confess their sins, so he becomes a Timothy Leary-type guru. Courtney's friend Peter Link wrote the music and collaborated with him on the book and lyrics.

I produced *Salvation* at the Jan Hus Theater off-Broadway with the backing of Capitol Records. The *New York Times* theater critic Lawrence Van Gelder called *Salvation* "the son of *Hair.*" The cast album for *Salvation* took off when Ronnie Dyson, a star from the cast of *Hair*, recorded a song from the show called "(If You Let Me Make Love to You Then) Why Can't I Touch You?" In 1970, it sold more than a million copies and was No. 8 on the charts around the world.

After the first six months that *Salvation* played in New York, I needed a replacement for one of the roles. I hired a young singer with an amazing voice and paid her $75 a week. Her name was Bette

Midler. I paid the assistant pianist on the show $35 a week, and his name was Barry Manilow.

* * *

I had been in show business for ten years and during that time I had produced 15 shows. I made money from three of them, *The Impossible Years, George M!* and *Cabaret.* During that time I had helped launch the careers of Burt Reynolds, Jerry Orbach, Gene Hackman, Brenda Vaccaro, Estelle Parsons, Olympia Dukakis, Bernadette Peters, Bette Midler, and Barry Manilow. I should have stopped producing and started managing all this new talent!

Salvation ran for 239 performances in New York and earned a net profit of $55,000, half of which went to me. The other half went to Capitol Records in return for financing the show. Capitol also earned royalties from the songs whenever they were played, and Ronnie Dyson's record company made millions from his recording of "(If You Let Me Make Love to You Then) Why Can't I Touch You?" Once again, I was the low man on the totem pole when it came to getting paid for my efforts.

I took my mother-in-law to see a play in the basement of a hotel in Boston. There were 14 people in the audience. My mother-in-law laughed, so I decided to produce it. The play was called *The Knack.* As Mel Gussow described it in the *Times* many years later, "A young man of rebellious instinct is painting his new basement flat. Helping and hindering him are two friends and fellow tenants, one a shy schoolteacher, who is the building's landlord, the other a narcissistic Don Juan, who has only one purpose, to entrap every attractive woman who crosses his path." The play was written by an English playwright, Ann Jellico, but no one had done anything about it for 16 years. Mike Nichols was becoming known for his direction of fast-paced comedy so I decided to show him the script. Mike told me he would like to direct it off-Broadway but he said he did not think it would be successful on Broadway.

Salvation had taught me how hard it is to make money off-Broadway, even with a hit, so I decided to let Mike Nichols direct *The Knack* off-Broadway if he could find another producer. My only condition was that I receive billing, which said, "Produced by arrangement with David Black." I hoped this gesture might persuade Mike to direct a show for me on Broadway someday. Mike found a producer who gave me my billing as legally required, but it was printed in type so small you couldn't read it.

The Knack was not only a money-making success off-Broadway, but Richard Lester directed a hugely successful film of it in between *A Hard Day's Night* and *Help,* the two films he directed for the Beatles.

Sol Hurok called me from London where he had seen a hilarious revue, written by a group of comic writer-performers at the University of Cambridge. As he had promised me after *Look, We've Come Through!* Hurok said he would provide all the financing needed to produce the show on Broadway. He also told me it was the first time he had ever shared producing credit with anyone. Walter Kerr's review in the *New York Times* said the writers of *Cambridge Circus* should stick around and teach American playwrights how to write comedy. No one had ever heard of John Cleese or Graham Chapman so the show was not a success, but a year later they became known all over the world as the creators of Monty Python. Once again, I had contributed to the success of great talent and not shared in the profits.

Before *Cambridge Circus* closed, I was invited to be a guest on *The Ed Sullivan Show* with John Cleese and Graham Chapman. When

Ed asked me, "What does a Broadway producer do?" I answered, "When I find out I will let you know."

* * *

I promised another young man he could have his name next to mine as the co-producer of a play called *Paris Is Out!* if he could come up with $70, 000, which was half of the financing. *Paris Is Out!* concerned a couple who were planning a trip to Europe and whenever the wife mentioned Paris, the husband said, "Paris is out!" The stars were Molly Picon and Sam Levene from the Yiddish Theater. The play received weak notices and I realized I would have to close it. When I broke the news to my co-producer he said, "David, what should I do now?"

"Why don't you try real estate?" I suggested.

The young man's name was Donald Trump.

Paris Is Out! was my 16th Broadway show. Four of them had made money, which meant my batting average was .250, fine for professional baseball but on Broadway it meant that every time I produced a new show the odds were four to one it would be a flop. With each new show, I was becoming more and more nervous. I spent opening nights in the nearest bar, unable to watch what was happening on the stage. At the opening-night parties at Sardi's, everyone was happy and drunk until the press agent appeared and told me the reviews were not good. Then, it was up to me to break the news to the investors. Suddenly, the party became a wake.

The morning after *Paris Is Out!* closed, there was a deathly silence in my office. I called it "the four-wall disease." My phone did not ring and I sat staring at the walls trying to figure out what to do next. It was 1970 and I had not had a hit for three years.

A brilliant idea! A brilliant idea! That's what I need, a brilliant idea.

It was Zero Mostel's famous line from *A Funny Thing Happened on the Way to the Forum*. My subconscious was speaking to me — *A Funny Thing Happened on the Way to the Forum* was the perfect show! It was funny and sexy and it had a beautiful score by Stephen Sondheim. The starring role of Pseudolus, the Roman slave, was not originally written for Zero Mostel. It was written for Phil Silvers, who had never played it! And Phil Silvers was a bigger name than Zero Mostel because he was Sgt. Bilko on TV!

Why not produce a show that is guaranteed to be a hit?

Phil Silvers agreed to star in my revival of *A Funny Thing Happened on the Way to the Forum*. We assembled a cast of hilarious comedians and voluptuous women and Steve Sondheim wrote two new songs. When we opened in Chicago we were an instant hit and when we opened in New York, Clive Barnes, writing in the *New York Times*, said, "Everyone ought to have a favorite Broadway musical. Personally, my favorite has been *A Funny Thing Happened on the Way to the Forum*. Last night at the Lunt-Fontanne Theater *A Funny Thing* happened once again, and I fell in love with it as desperately as ever. This is the funniest, bawdiest, and most enchanting Broadway musical ever."

Despite Clive's review, no one came to the box office. No one bought tickets. "I can't believe this," I said to Jose Vega, my veteran stage manager. "A funny, sexy musical with a big star and great reviews! Why is no one buying tickets?"

"There's a big dance in Newark," said Jose.

"What does that mean?"

"It means," said Jose, "that on Broadway you never know why you have a hit or why you have a flop."

My revival of *A Funny Thing Happened on the Way to the Forum* closed and lost $500,000. It was my third flop in a row. According to my batting average my next show would be a hit.

I received a phone call from Michael Cacoyannis, who had just won the Oscar for directing Anthony Quinn in *Zorba the Greek*.

"Mr. Black," said Cacoyannis, "I understand you are the only honest producer on Broadway." That wasn't saying much because there were only eight of us who were working as independent producers at the time. Cacoyannis told me he had written a musical version of the Greek play *Lysistrata*, where the women refuse to have sex with their husbands unless they stop the war. He had Melina Mercouri to star. She had just become world-famous for her role as the prostitute in the film *Never on Sunday*. Melina was one of those actresses who could sell out a theater reading the telephone book.

Cacoyannis needed someone to write the music and $600,000. I raised the money and got *Salvation* composer Peter Link to compose the score. When we were in previews at The Brooks Atkinson Theater with *Lysistrata*, I eavesdropped on the audience conversations in the intermission and they were discussing their golf handicaps. This was not a good sign.

Cacoyannis said he had a brilliant idea that would make the show a hit. He told me to walk over to Sutton Place South at midnight after the show, and look straight up in the air. As I stood on the darkened street corner, a window opened high up in one of the apartment buildings. I wondered if Cacoyannis was planning to jump. Instead of Cacoyannis, a white bird flew out of the window and made circles over my head. When it finally landed at my feet, I discovered it was a realistic replica of a white dove with a motor in its tail.

I took the elevator up to the 30th floor of the building and there was Cacoyannis sitting on his couch, surrounded by 500 mechanical doves he had ordered at my expense from Paris. He told me he was planning to let some of the doves loose in the audience at the end of each performance and he said he had ordered 500 because he knew we were in for a long run.

Lysistrata closed in one night and lost $950,000, and I was served with a lawsuit by a member of the audience; one of the doves had hit him in the eye.

* * *

It was 1972 and *Lysistrata* was my 18th Broadway show. If I was going to continue raising huge sums of money to find out what the *New York Times* critic thought of my show, I wanted to be personally responsible for what was happening on the stage. I had employed many of the theater's most talented directors — Joshua Logan, Mike Nichols, Margaret Webster, Jose Quintero, Sir John Gielgud, Burt Shevelove, and Joe Layton — and I had learned enough to want to make my own mistakes. I made a rule: I would no longer produce a show unless I also directed it.

* * *

On August 7, 1974, I went to see Rudolf Nureyev dance in *Swan Lake* at the Metropolitan Opera House. As I walked across Lincoln Square, I remembered the first time my grandfather took me to an opera at the Met. Then I thought about my experiences as an extra at the Met and my audition for Boris Goldovsky. Now, I was going to the Met to watch the most famous ballet dancer in the world.

While I was thinking these thoughts, I walked by the line waiting for returned tickets for the sold-out performance of *Swan*

Lake, and a young woman said hello as if she knew me. I had a vague memory of meeting her. Then, I heard myself say, "If you get a ticket, let's have a drink in the intermission." At the end of the first act of *Swan Lake*, Anne Rivers walked out of the box next to mine and into my life.

I had met Anne at a piano recital at a friend's home in Wilton, Connecticut. I was chatting up a wealthy Greek investor and Anne had offered me some fruit. I had smiled at her and gone on with my pitch.

When we walked out of the Met at the end of *Swan Lake*, Anne said she had a premonition she would see me again. She told me she loved the ballet, so I took off my shoe and showed her my arch.

* * *

At this point, Linda and I were doing our best to raise Sophie and her two brothers, Sandor and Jeremy. Sandor was rushing everywhere, and Jeremy was proceeding more philosophically. Having children had not solved our marriage problems. We were no longer defying our fathers but over the years our personalities had developed in different directions and we had grown apart. During the week, I was a Broadway producer and on weekends, we were immersed in the challenges of raising a family.

When I met Anne at *Swan Lake*, I was in rehearsal with a play I was directing off-Broadway called *The Advertisement*, which had starred Derek Jacobi and Joan Plowright in London. Off-Broadway producers dream about producing on Broadway, and if they can get a Broadway producer to direct one of their shows, their dream might come true. For me, it was a chance to pursue a directing career while someone else supplied the financing.

In addition to directing, my audition seminars were becoming popular. My original purpose had been to learn why actors give great auditions but are often incapable of repeating their performance in a full production. During my seminars, I learned that acting and auditioning are two different skills. The actor is a magician. He convinces us he is someone else and he makes us care about this imaginary person. But the actor has help when he performs his magic. He has sets, lights, and costumes, and an audience that has paid to watch him. When the actor goes to audition, there are no sets, lights, or costumes, and the only audience he has is the producer and the creative team who are usually more nervous than he is.

During my seminars I invented a technique for auditioning that was helping actors get jobs. My audition technique was based on creating substitutes for the missing elements that usually help an actor create his magic, so that the audition audience gets to have the same experience as the audience in a theater.

There are four different kinds of auditions. In each one, the actor must find a way to compensate for a different missing element. In the monologue audition, the missing element is another actor to listen to; in the cold reading, the actor has not read the script so he doesn't have a goal to achieve; in the musical audition, there is the same missing element as in the monologue audition: another actor to react to; and in the audition interview, there is no script so the actor has to invent one.

When Anne walked into my life, I wasn't bored or looking for a new relationship, but something undeniable had happened. A beautiful swan had appeared on Tchaikovsky's lake and was gliding in my direction. There was nothing I could do about it. When we walked out of *Swan Lake* together, a new life was beginning. I wanted to play a leading role in Anne's life, so I would have to have a successful audition.

Anne was born in Cornwall, England. When she was four, her parents immigrated to Australia as farmers. Ten years later, they returned to England and by the time Anne was 18, she had settled in New York. When we met, Anne was 29 and I was 43. Anne told me she had been looking forward to spending time on her own after separating from her husband. *Swan Lake* changed that. Our relationship was growing into something we could never have imagined. It was happening by itself without any effort on our part, and I knew Anne would not wait forever for me to do something about my marriage.

* * *

I felt the need to impress Anne by having her watch me produce a Broadway show. Since that was not possible anymore, I did the next best thing: I took Anne to dinner at Sardi's, the famous restaurant where I had hosted so many opening-night parties. While I was telling Anne stories of Broadway, a voice in the next booth called out, "David, old chap! How are you?"

It was Dan Crawford, the director of The King's Head Theatre in London. Dan spoke with a perfect English accent although he came from Hackensack, New Jersey.

"I was just thinking of you, old boy!" said Dan. "We have a huge hit in London and I am looking for someone to produce it on Broadway! It's a musical and it's called *Fearless Frank*. It's based on the life of the famous Irish writer Frank Harris. The star is Britain's favorite song-and-dance man, Niall Toibin, and he is willing to come to Broadway!"

The King's Head Theatre had launched the careers of many well-known actors, directors, and playwrights, and Dan had invited me to direct a new American play called *Shay* at his theater where it had been a success. While Dan was talking, I became excited.

Here is a chance for Anne to see me produce a Broadway show!

Then I remembered my new rule not to produce anything unless I also directed it.

"Niall Toibin will only star with Robert Gillespie as director," said Dan, anticipating my thoughts, "because Gillespie made *Fearless Frank* a hit."

If Fearless Frank *is already a hit, my rule does not apply and I can produce it on Broadway!*

By this time, Dan Crawford had joined us in our booth at Sardi's, and Anne was smiling.

Zinsky at the Waldorf

During dinner at Sardi's, Dan Crawford told us the producer of *Fearless Frank* in London was Oscar Lewenstein, David Merrick's English co-conspirator in the bidding war for the rights to *Semi-Detached*. Dan said Oscar would be supplying half of the financing for *Fearless Frank* on Broadway and he would have billing as co-producer, but I would have final say in all decisions.

Since *Fearless Frank* was already a hit in London, it was easy to raise my half of the financing. Oscar flew to New York for the first day of rehearsals. Over lunch at Sardi's, he filled me in on the colorful life of the real Frank Harris who was born in Ireland in 1856. Harris was an editor, journalist, and publisher who hobnobbed with the most talented and famous figures of his day, including Oscar Wilde and George Bernard Shaw. He had lived all over the world, including America, where he worked as a cowboy, and was known for his irascible, aggressive personality. His biggest success was his memoir, *My Life and Loves*, which was banned around the world because of its sexual content.

Oscar told me the key to portraying Frank Harris on stage was a larger-than-life energy. He said Niall Toibin had plenty of energy in the London production, but he was concerned that it was missing from what he'd seen so far in New York. Oscar had discussed this problem with Bob Gillespie, our director, and he asked me to keep him informed.

During rehearsals, it seemed to me that Oscar's worries about Niall Tobin's lack of energy were justified, but when I discussed it with Bob Gillespie he said Niall was one of those actors who needed an audience. Opening night of *Fearless Frank* was sold out and the audience was enthusiastic, but it seemed to me that Niall did not rise to the occasion.

My therapist invested in *Fearless Frank*. I didn't want her to but I was afraid to say no. She came to the opening night party at Sardi's. While we were waiting for the reviews, I took some of her nervous pills. After the reviews came out, I took some of her perk-me-up pills. The next morning, I realized I had made a big mistake. I had been upset because of the bad reviews.

Great reviews, great stars, and great directors don't mean any-thing! But there is a key to success on Broadway, after all! It was right under my nose all the time! The key to success on Broadway is the pro-ducer! Producers have special insights. That's why they are producers! Producers know what will be a success without relying on anyone else, and I know that Fearless Frank *will be a hit. All I have to do is keep it running!*

My stage manager told me the cast was giving sloppy perfor-mances because there were only a few people in the audience. I gave a pep talk to the cast. "This show will be a hit! People will forget the reviews. We are getting great word of mouth!" I sat in the theater and yelled *Bravo!* at the end of each performance.

My business manager told me no one was buying tickets. He said he needed money to pay the cast and the theater. My lawyer told me I would be personally liable for any unpaid bills. My friends told me to close the show. No one believed that *Fearless Frank* would be a hit. That was because they did not know about my intuitive powers.

Laurence Olivier knew, and so did Donald Trump. Both of them asked for my advice. Even the president of the United States knew. That's why he was nervous talking to me. I need to get away from unen-lightened people who are sabotaging my work.

I checked into the Waldorf Astoria under the name of Morton Zinsky. I didn't want anyone to know where I was. That included my therapist. I was doing this for her own good. I had to keep

Fearless Frank running because she had invested in it. My suite at the Waldorf was located on the eighth floor between the entrance flags overlooking Park Avenue. My broker was Merrill Lynch and they had their offices directly opposite the Waldorf, on the other side of Park Avenue. Whenever I needed money, I stood in the window and waved. Then, I held up fingers to indicate how much money I needed. Lately, I had been waving a lot because I needed $100,000 to keep *Fearless Frank* running.

I could see deeper meanings in everything. Numbers had special significance. Words and names had double meanings. Opposites were the same. I knew where my intuitive powers came from. They came from my father.

My father is God and I am the son of God!

Special things always happen to me at the Waldorf. This is where I received the statue of myself as the Salesman of the Year in the Grand Ballroom. Now, something of even greater importance is about to occur. I have already produced a show for the president of the United States and 10,000 people. Now, I am about to make theater history. Fearless Frank *will be the biggest hit that Broadway has ever seen!*

My struggle to make Fearless Frank *a hit will be an Oscar-winning movie. It will be called* Zinsky at the Waldorf — How I Became Fearless and Frank on Broadway.

I need to keep track of everything for the screenplay. I recorded my telephone calls. I taped meetings and rehearsals. I kept my tape recorder running all night in case I said something of importance in my sleep.

In a nearby office building, a woman named Joan Feeley was transcribing the tapes I had made, and down in the hotel's vault three safe-deposit boxes held the tapes and transcriptions of all my meetings and telephone conversations since I had moved into the

Waldorf. Hidden behind the clothes in one of the closets in my suite was a box filled with earlier transcriptions Feeley had made, along with copies of them in separate envelopes. These papers were awaiting a fourth safe-deposit box.

The original title of my screenplay was *Freud on Broadway*. I had been producing Broadway shows for 20 years and I had been in therapy for 23, and I figured the combination was unusual. Lately, I had been turning my conferences with Bob Gillespie into therapy sessions. After 50 minutes I said, "We have to stop now."

* * *

I didn't want anyone to steal my story, so I paid for Morton Zinsky's suite to be under 24-hour surveillance by a hidden camera and I hired a security guard to sit in the hall.

I was sleeping three hours a night, which gave me more time to make *Fearless Frank* a hit. I grew a beard so I wouldn't have to waste time shaving. I ate chocolate bars, smoked cigars, and tripled the dose of the perk-me-up pills. I was losing weight but I felt great. I called Clive Barnes, who had reviewed *Fearless Frank* for the *New York Times*. I reached him in China, where he was covering a ballet.

"Clive, I'd be willing to pay for your first-class air fare if you would fly home and write a second opinion. What? What?"

I couldn't understand what Clive was saying. He sounded annoyed about something. I tried to sleep but even with two different sleeping pills I had no success. I kept thinking about Frank Harris. I could hear him singing his opening number, "The Man Who Made His Life into a Work of Art." Then, I remembered Frank Harris had died in 1931, the year I was born.

Maybe I am *Frank Harris!*

A few days later, the buzzer sounded on the door to my suite. Someone had broken my cover. Maybe it was Clive! When I opened the door, there was Anne, my therapist, and my family doctor. "David," said Anne, "you look exhausted. We have some pills that will help you sleep and see things more clearly."

I was in love with Anne but I didn't trust her. She didn't understand what it meant to be a Broadway producer. I didn't trust my therapist, either. She had been giving me four different pills. As long as I was Zinsky at the Waldorf, I didn't have to take any of them. My family doctor was someone I did trust. He had taken care of me since I was a teenager. He was not keen on therapists in general—mine in particular.

It was strange to see these three people together. While I was trying to think of something to say, I passed out.

* * *

I woke up five days later in my apartment. I had been having a nightmare about someone named Morton Zinsky. Anne told me I looked like Howard Hughes, skinny with a beard, long fingernails, and bags under my eyes. I shaved off my beard and ate and slept for several weeks. As soon as I felt better, I felt worse. I was terrified to get out of bed. Another few days as Morton Zinsky and I would have to be hospitalized!

I knew I should leave my therapist. I had been her patient for 23 years and I had learned why she was the cheapest therapist in town. When I told her I wanted to leave, she said, "I want you to have electroshock treatments. If that doesn't work, there's nothing else I can do for you." I was not in a hurry to have shock treatments, but I felt as if part of my brain had already disappeared. It was the part that loved theater and music. I was also afraid I might become Morton Zinsky again. I had to do something.

Anne took me to the hospital for the shock treatments. I was nervous before each treatment, but afterwards I had a strange new feeling of peace.

* * *

I found a new therapist who said I was Bipolar Type II with mild highs and occasional lows. It sounded like a weather report. He told me I became Morton Zinsky because of all of the different drugs my old therapist had prescribed for me to take at the same time. He said it would never happen again. I couldn't think of anything to say to my new therapist, so I made a drawing of him. When I got home, I was amazed. The drawing looked exactly like him!

After closing *Fearless Frank* and paying Morton Zinsky's bill at the Waldorf, my finances were at an all-time low. Then I received a phone call from Albert Bush Brown, the Chancellor of Long Island University. He told me they had just built a $2 million theater on the campus of C.W. Post on Long Island. It was called the Concert Theater and they were looking for someone to run it. He offered me the position of Theater Director with a staff of ten and a salary for two years. My job was to fill the theater with the greatest orchestras, singers, and instrumentalists in the world, so the people of Long Island would not have to travel to Manhattan for classical music. I accepted.

I spent most of my time as Director of the Concert Theater haggling over the price of well-known talent with Columbia Artists Management Inc.

"Tell you what," said the CAMI agent over lunch at his favorite restaurant, "the Boston Symphony Orchestra is going to cost you $50,000, including Ozawa. Take the Danish Ballet's *Swan Lake* for $15,000, and I'll reduce the price of the BSO to $40,000. Let's say $60,000 for the package! If your budget permits, I'll throw in Pavarotti for another $25,000."

I came away from these lunches depressed and with indigestion. The depression came from bargaining over the price of priceless music. The indigestion came from eating the meat at the agent's favorite restaurant.

* * *

I was still conducting my audition seminars at the New School, and one day, Lewis Falb, the director of the theater department, suggested I make the seminars into a book. When I said there must be many books on the subject of auditioning, Falb said, "Yes, but yours will be the only book ever written by a producer!" He suggested I take a look at what was out there.

I went to the Drama Book Shop and asked the owner about books on auditioning. He said there was one book that aspiring actors bought as soon as they arrived at the bus terminal in Manhattan. I looked at the book, which was written by a casting director. In the introduction, he wrote, "Auditioning and acting are two different skills."

This is what I discovered so I don't need to write my book.

Then, in the next paragraph I read, "Everything in this book that applies to auditioning also applies to acting." I decided to write my book.

The Actor's Audition was published in 1990.

Lewis Falb also told me there were 500 seats in the main auditorium of the New School, which were empty on Monday nights. He asked me if I could fill them. My audition technique was based on showing the actor how to become someone else without sets, lights, costumes, and an audience. Now, I needed to learn how the actor performs his magic when the actor gets all the help he needs.

We called the new course "The Magic of Theater." Thirty-three of America's best-known actors agreed to donate their Monday evenings for four semesters in the main auditorium of the New School. This became a revealing exploration into the magic of live theater. Among the actors who participated were F. Murray Abraham, Alan Arkin, Claire Bloom, Charles Busch, Zoe Caldwell, Stockard Channing, Hume Cronyn, Jim Dale, Colleen Dewhurst, Elizabeth Franz, Joel Grey, Julie Harris, William Hurt, Judith Ivey, Madeline Kahn, Swoosie Kurtz, Frank Langella, Anne Meara, Kate Nelligan, Amanda Plummer, Tony Randall, Christopher Reeve, Maureen Stapleton, Elaine Stritch, Jessica Tandy, Liv Ullmann, Christopher Walken, and Eli Wallach.

I talked with two actors in each session. Some of them I had worked with and some I was meeting for the first time. Before each session I picked them up with a car and driver and took them for tea or a drink in a little restaurant behind the New School's auditorium. The relaxed atmosphere of the almost empty, dimly lit restaurant had the womblike quality of a dressing room. Instead of wishing the actors luck with their performances as a producer, I was now sharing the stage with them. My first two guests were Joel Grey and Julie Harris. Just before we made our entrance, Joel put his arm around me and told me, "Don't worry, everything will be fine."

While preparing for "The Magic of Theater," I reviewed the history of theater going back to its beginnings in ancient Greece, when Thespis first stepped out of the chorus. I discovered that in 1888 an Englishman named William Archer sent out a questionnaire to the leading actors of his day, including Sarah Bernhardt. Archer was the translator of Henrik Ibsen, whose naturalistic dramas were being performed in London for the first time. At the top of his questionnaire Archer wrote, "To Feel or Not to Feel? That Is the Question." Archer wanted to settle the debate over who had the greater effect on the audience: the actor who feels an emotion or the actor who imitates it. He published the results in a book called *Masks or Faces? A Study in the Psychology of Acting*. In the end, William Archer concluded that there should be a compromise between the two positions, but he also wrote, "Someday, perhaps, a better psychologist may tread the maze to its inmost recesses."

It had been 100 years since Archer's book. I got hold of his questionnaire and asked the same questions of my well-known guests. What happened on each of those evenings was unique and, like an evening at a play, will never occur in quite the same way again. It became the basis for my second book, *The Magic of Theater*.

* * *

Meanwhile, despite my days as Morton Zinsky, I found myself missing the experience of live theater. Not having control over the creative process as a producer had driven me to the brink, but directing by itself was still a possibility. One day, I strolled down Fifty-Fourth Street and introduced myself to the head of the American Theater of Actors. He handed me the script of a new play called *The Guys in the Truck*, about a bunch of men televising a football game from a remote-control truck. The play was written by a sportscaster at CBS.

I assembled a no-name cast and rehearsed for a month. The *New York Times* theater critic Mel Gussow showed up for the opening and wrote a "money" review. The next morning, people were lined up around the block waiting to buy tickets. The show was sold out for six months in advance, but the theater was losing money because there were ten people in the cast and only 54 seats in the theater. If I closed the play, I would lose my first review as a director in the *New York Times*. To keep *The Guys in the Truck* running, I decided to move it to Broadway. Since I was also directing, I would not be breaking my rule.

* * *

The budget for the off-off-Broadway production of *The Guys in the Truck* was $350 a week so the actors could eat lunch on stage in full view of the audience. The budget for the Broadway production was $950,000, and to raise that kind of money I needed a star. Once again, I found myself in Hollywood showing the script to my former acting classmate Jack Lemmon, Jack Klugman, and to Gene Hackman, whom I had already employed in *Look, We've Come Through!* All of them were interested in playing the lead in a film but none wanted to take a chance on Broadway. Elliott Gould was in the middle of a quiet spell and he read a few lines for me in his living room. The lure of Broadway took over once again, and I forgot everything I had learned about auditioning and hired him on the spot.

I found a theater, and raised the $950,000, but after five days of rehearsals I discovered I couldn't hear Elliott Gould beyond the eighth row. I fired him and gave the leading role to his understudy, Harris Laskaway, who had played the lead in the original production. When I fired Elliott Gould, *The Guys in the Truck* received the kind of publicity Broadway producers dream about. The *Daily News* had a picture of Gould on the front page with the headline, "Producer Throws Guy off His Truck!"

On opening night of the Broadway production of *The Guys in the Truck*, Mel Gussow brought his ten-year-old sports-loving son along to see the same cast in the same play he had raved about in the *New York Times*. At the beginning of his new review Gussow mentioned that underneath the name of Harris Laskaway on the marquee you could see that someone had painted over the name of Elliott Gould. The cautious theatergoing public stayed home and *The Guys in the Truck* closed in one night and lost $950,000.

When *Lysistrata* closed in one night and lost $950,000, I made a rule I would no longer produce a show unless I also directed it. When *The Guys in the Truck* closed in one night and lost $950,000, I made a second rule: I would not produce and direct at the same time. Twenty-three years of producing Broadway shows were gone forever from my life.

* * *

I was depressed. I lay on my bed in Stonington, Connecticut, and thought of Jose Ferrer as Toulouse-Lautrec in the film, *Moulin Rouge*. Lautrec is dying and the Can-Can girls are walking by his bed waving goodbye. At the foot of *my* bed I saw Laurence Olivier, Julie Andrews, David Merrick, Bette Midler, Barry Manilow, Joel Grey, Gene Hackman, Richard Nixon, Donald Trump, and Bernadette Peters waving goodbye. Then Boris Goldovsky appeared. "Mr. Blek," said Goldovsky, "haff you zoht of trying zomzing else?"

The Garbage Strike

It was summer and I was walking in the village of Stonington, with its 300-year-old houses and 200-year-old trees. I could not believe that Broadway was gone forever from my life. Where would I ever have adventures that would equal opening nights at Sardi's? I wanted my friends to know what had happened, so I wrote a story and illustrated it with drawings.

THE STORY OF DAVID

1983

DAVID SPENT THE FIRST SIX MONTHS OF THE YEAR RAISING MONEY FOR HIS BROADWAY SHOW. IT CLOSED IN ONE NIGHT.

HIS CLOSEST RELATIVES COULDN'T HELP.

HIS FATHER PUFFED ON HIS PIPE.

HIS MOTHER SLEPT ON HER COUCH.

THEN THEY WENT AWAY.

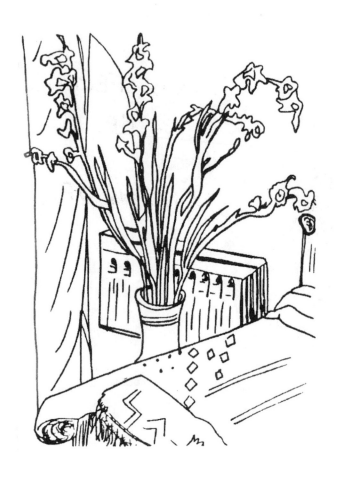

HIS GIRL TOOK OFF FOR AN INDIAN
RESERVATION LEAVING NOTHING BUT
FLOWERS ON HER SIDE OF THE BED.

DAVID FELT LIKE HE WAS CRACKING UP.

HIS BROTHER WAS SAD BUT
HAD NO ADVICE.

HIS SON FROM HARVARD TRIED TO THINK
OF SOMETHING.

HIS THERAPIST HAD
"NO COMMENT."

SO DAVID DECIDED TO LEAVE THE CITY
AND SPEND THE SUMMER IN A LITTLE
TOWN BY THE SEA.

HE LED A SIMPLE LIFE.

HE LISTENED TO OTHER PEOPLE'S
CONVERSATIONS.

HE MADE NEW FRIENDS.

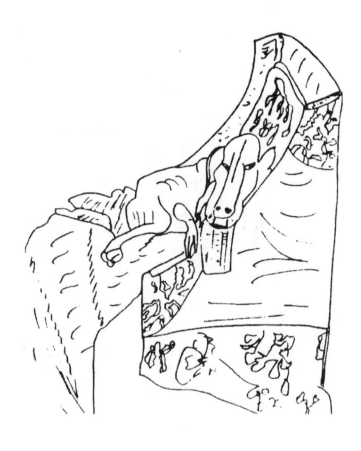

HE TOOK TIME TO GET TO
KNOW ANIMALS.

HE WATCHED GIRLS ON THE BEACH.

HE MET PEOPLE WITH A NOSE
FOR THE SEA.

HE KEPT UP WITH WORLD EVENTS.

HE GOT TO KNOW PEOPLE WHO WERE
RELAXED AND PHILOSOPHICAL.

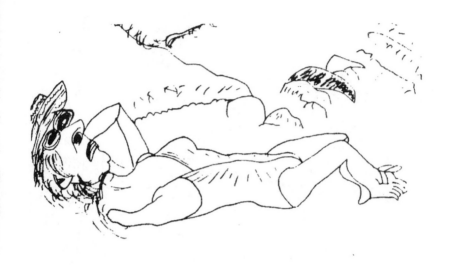

THEN ONE DAY HIS GIRL RETURNED
LOOKING LIKE A CELEBRITY.

THE NIGHTS BEGAN TO TURN COOL.

SO DAVID DECIDED TO RETURN TO THE
CITY.

HE LUNCHED WITH HIS AGENT.

HE ATTENDED CONCERTS,

WENT TO CLUBS,

PARTIES,

AND BAR MITZVAHS.

HE VISITED HIS USUAL HAUNTS

AND SAW OLD FRIENDS.

OTHERS BEGAN TO TELL HIS STORY.

HE FELT AT HOME AGAIN AMONG
SOPHISTICATED PEOPLE.

EVERYTHING SEEMED BACK TO NORMAL...

Anne and I sent my story to our friends. One of Anne's friends was living with a well-known English artist in London named Patrick Caulfield. Anne received a phone call from her friend, Janet Nathan, saying Patrick and John Hoyland, another English artist, from London's Royal Academy of Arts, wanted to meet me. Anne was going to visit her family in London so I went with her to meet the artists.

Patrick Caulfield and John Hoyland told me my drawings were unusual. John said they were "quirky and arresting" and he liked their "twitchy edginess." He said my line had "a life of its own" regardless of the subject, and "that is what real drawing is all about." John told me I could have a career as an artist. I was excited. When I asked John who I should study with, he said, "Nobody. There are a lot of bad teachers out there and you might get one. Stick to your own bad habits!" John also told me I was lucky to have become an artist at this point in my life because I wouldn't have to go through "the painful unlearning process" he had to go through before he could find his artistic identity. John's words reminded me of my experience in theater, where the actors with the most training often have the hardest time expressing themselves.

John Hoyland and Patrick Caulfield suggested I start painting. I bought paints, brushes, an easel, and some canvas, and drove into the country. I saw a red barn on a green hill and set up my easel. I squeezed out red and green paint and picked up a brush.

Come on, barn. Come on, hill! Come on, barn. Come on, hill! Slowly, very slowly, the barn and the hill began to appear.

I found a spot by a river. While I was painting, I forgot where I was and what day it was. The sights and sounds and smells of the country were flowing through my body onto the canvas. I was experiencing the essence of art! Just at this moment, a woman walked by with her son and stopped to look at my painting. "Look at the nice man painting, dear! Just like you do in kindergarten!"

* * *

I wanted to learn about great art so I visited the Barnes Foundation collection in Philadelphia. A sign at the entrance said, "The great art of the past is alive because it embodies the ideas and feelings of talented men in universal and eternal themes." While I was looking at Cezanne's portrait of his wife, the woman next to me said, "Looks like he painted her hair on a bad day." In front of a Renoir, I heard, "How would you know those are chrysanthemums? They look like blobs of paint!" While I was looking at Matisse's *The Music Lesson*, someone said, "He must have been in a hurry when he did this."

There must be more to great art than meets the eye.

I did a painting of some women bathing in the Ganges at sunrise from a photograph I had taken when I was in India with my parents. Their colorful saris were floating in the river. The painting was creating itself. I was watching my brushstrokes make it happen. It was a magical experience. After two hours, I stopped and looked at the painting and I was horrified. The women's heads were too big. Their arms and legs looked like tree trunks. Everything was distorted! I was angry and embarrassed, so I threw the painting out with the garbage. The next morning I went to collect the empty garbage pail, but the garbage pail was still full, and my painting was still there. When I asked the superintendent of our building what was happening, he said, "There's a garbage strike." I had to bring the painting back into our apartment.

One hour later, Sir Frederick Gore, Head of the Exhibitions Committee for London's Royal Academy of Arts, came to look at my work at the suggestion of Patrick Caulfield and John Hoyland. He looked at my paintings and said, "I am going to give you an exhibition in London, and we will have that one there, the one leaning against the wall with the wet paint. What's it called?"

"Uh... *Indian Bathers*."

* * *

Ray Rushton, the critic for England's *Arts Review* came to my exhibition in London and wrote, "Mr. Black's inspirational approach works when design combines with color intensity in *Indian Bathers*, where the overall pattern of figures strongly suggests the exotic generosity of Hindu Temple carving."

Indian Bathers was sold to the vice-president of Lloyd's of London.

Another of my paintings, *Rhododendrons and Azaleas*, was sold to a New York collector who wanted to know where I had painted it. I had created the painting from a photograph I cut out of a magazine. The curator for my exhibition in London told me I had painted the legendary home of Sir Edmund de Rothschild, head of the English branch of the Rothschild family. It was called Exbury Gardens and was located in Southampton. He said the gardens were visited by thousands of people every month and were celebrated all over the world for their unrivalled collection of rhododendrons and azaleas. The curator invited Sir Edmund himself to the exhibition. After I was back in America, I heard that Sir Edmund had seen the painting and confirmed that I had painted his gardens.

Shortly after Sir Edmund's visit to my exhibition, he sent an invitation to me and Anne to be his guests at Exbury Gardens the next time we came to England. Several months later, we found ourselves sitting in the rooms where the Rothschilds had entertained

Queen Elizabeth and Winston Churchill, among others. We had cocktails with Sir Edmund and Anne Rothschild in the Peacock Room, with its view of peacocks on the lawn and the Isle of Wight in the distance, and we ate dinner with Sir Edmund and his wife at the long table that had been used for the planning of D-Day. The superb Rothschild wines were poured from silver pitchers that could have financed the invasion.

Before retiring, Sir Edmund gave me a map so I could find the exact location of the rhododendrons and azaleas I had painted. At six the next morning, I walked into the magical place I had recreated but never seen.

* * *

Frederick Gore, "Freddy," invited me to paint with him in Provence near his summer home in Bonnieux. We sat next to each other in an olive-tree orchard, surrounded by orange-brown earth, and the white mountains of les Alpilles in the distance, where Dante composed his *Inferno*. Freddy was creating a masterpiece with perfect perspective and amazing colors. I was concentrating on the colors of the earth and the mountains and treating the olive trees more lightly.

"You can't get away with that!" said Freddy. "The trunks of your olive trees look like crow's feet!"

I took a brush and began thickening the trunks.

"What are you doing?" asked Freddy.

"I am getting rid of the crow's feet."

"Leave it exactly as it is!" said Freddy. "Some people might like it!"

"The problem for the modern painter is to make an arrangement where shapes and colors and lines are important and interesting," Freddy continued, "regardless of what the painting is about. The colors and harmonies must be exciting and at the same time say something. Try and make your painting correspond to a personal experience!"

Freddy was giving me the same advice I gave to actors when they had to audition with a script they had never seen! In the "cold reading," the actor must invent a story in order to be believable. When I looked at the olive trees, I noticed that each of them was closely surrounded by two other trees. I imagined I was an olive tree forced to live with my parents for the next 200 years.

"You're beginning to get the knack of it," said Freddy. "Your painting is coming to life!"

Freddy had been the head teacher at St. Martin's School of Painting for 28 years. He had rescued my painting of *Indian Bathers* from the garbage and launched my painting career. In his introduction to my exhibition in London, Freddy wrote, "David Black is a serious painter and his paintings are fun. He paints what he likes, he paints what he has seen and he paints it with a sure sense of comedy, really wild comedy, but just too perceptive and observant to be called satire. We can see how his background in the disciplines of the theater has sustained the development of an art so apparently innocent and intuitive."

* * *

When I returned from London, I did not know anyone in the New York art world. My friends suggested I look for a gallery with paintings that looked like mine.

"You're too painterly," said the owner of a gallery in Soho. "You belong on Madison Avenue."

"You know what pays my rent?" asked the owner of a Madison Avenue gallery. "Classical Realism! Classical Realism pays my rent. You're an Impressionist! You belong on Fifty-Seventh Street!"

"Do you know what you are doing?" asked the owner of a gallery on Fifty-Seventh Street.

"No, I don't."

"You're doing Outsider Art. Outsider Art is done by artists who are self-taught, they are emotionally disturbed, and they have been in prison."

I almost qualified for that one.

Upper-Middle-Class Schadenfreude

A young man named Rick Davidman bought the DFN Gallery in Soho and invited me to exhibit there. He published a catalog of the paintings in the exhibition and sent it to newspapers and magazines. One week before the opening reception, I asked his assistant if there had been any response.

"Nobody. Just someone from *The New Yorker*."

"Who was it?"

"I didn't get the name."

"What did they want?"

"They wanted to know if the paintings in the catalog would also be in the exhibition."

"Then what happened?"

"They sent a messenger over to pick up five catalogs."

Now I was excited and I asked a friend of mine in the art business what it meant. "It means they will probably review your show."

The next Monday, I was at my local newsstand at seven in the morning, waiting for *The New Yorker* to be delivered. There was no review but there was something called "The Short List for Soho." There were three names in bold: Willem de Kooning, Edward Hopper, and David Black. I was stunned. When I asked my friend what this meant, she said, "It means they will definitely review your show."

Three days later, Rick Davidman told me the art critic for *The New Yorker* had been to see my exhibition and liked it.

The following Monday, I read in *The New Yorker*:

"David Black – Wide-eyed tableaux of Upper-Middle-Class Schadenfreude (*The Benefit Dinner, The Costume Party, The Backer's Audition*) in appropriately sunny colors. The show offers several *plein-air* landscapes in homage to the marzipan light of France, but Black is at his most delicious as a satirist."

When I looked up the word *schadenfreude*, it said "enjoying other people's miseries."

On the Monday my review appeared in *The New Yorker*, I received a phone call from the magazine's art director. He asked me if I would do a self-portrait and hand it in by Thursday. I told him I didn't do self-portraits, and besides it would be a little wet.

"We're used to that."

I did a painting of myself reading my review in *The New Yorker* with a dog. When I brought it to *The New Yorker* office, I was greeted by the art staff, who thought my self-portrait was funny. However, the art director said there was a legal problem because I had reproduced *The New Yorker* cover. When I offered to change it, he said, "We don't like artists to tamper with their work."

My heart sank. By chance, I had brought along a painting of a close friend who looked like me. I had painted it in France during our visit to Van Gogh's night café.

"We will take that one," said the art director.

The following week, *David Black, Self-Portrait at the Night Café* appeared all by itself on a page in *The New Yorker*. As a result, I was offered exhibitions in Texas, Ohio, Connecticut, Rhode Island, California, and New Jersey. At the Museum of East Texas, the curator told me that the members wanted to know something about me. She suggested I give a short talk about myself at the opening reception. My talk lasted ten minutes but it got longer in Ohio and then longer in Connecticut. By the time I returned to New York, my talk lasted 45 minutes and had the title, "How Producing Broadway Shows Drove Me to a Painting Career."

Then, the president of The National Arts Club in New York invited me to give my talk in the Grand Gallery. He suggested I wear a tuxedo and circulate amongst the crowd while I was doing it. I realized if I was going to explain "How Producing Broadway Shows Drove Me to a Painting Career," I would also have to explain what drove me to produce Broadway shows. My one-person play, *Falling off Broadway*, was born.

* * *

It was Christmas, and Anne and I were in London to spend the holidays with her family. I was sitting in Hyde Park when a familiar voice said, "David, old boy, how are you?" It was Dan Crawford. The last time I had a conversation with Dan I had ended up as Zinsky at the Waldorf. Dan was still the director of The King's Head Theatre and when I told him about *Falling off Broadway*, he asked whether he could read the script. He called me on Christmas morning. "We go into rehearsal in four weeks and I am directing!"

Dan directed me in *Falling off Broadway* as if I was each of the characters, but I never lost my identity as the storyteller. I also had costume changes to fit what was happening. When I became a Broadway producer, I wore a swanky red-velvet smoking jacket to go with my cigar.

On opening night of *Falling off Broadway* at The King's Head Theatre, overtures from Broadway shows were playing on loud-speakers as the audience took their seats. While I was waiting back-stage, I could not believe I was about to appear on a stage in front of total strangers to tell the story of my life. It reminded me of waiting behind the sliding doors in my grandfather's living room before making my entrance in "The Greatest Show off Earth!"

I decided to take a peek at the audience and I saw a man sitting in the front row who looked exactly like my grandfather! He made me feel good and I was no longer nervous. After the show, I would have dinner with him. Then, I would light his cigar, and after my grandfather's cigar was lit he would tell me to put my finger on his nose. When I put my finger on my grandfather's nose, smoke would come out of his ears.

EPILOGUE

Here is what happened to the leading characters in this story:

President Nixon resigned and never asked me for tickets again.

Donald Trump took my advice.

My grandfather never gave any of his money away because he wanted the *New York Times* to print his net worth in his obituary. On the day he died, there was a newspaper strike.

My mother wrote her autobiography and never mentioned me. On her 80th birthday, I did a painting of her favorite flowers and wrote on the back, "Happy Birthday! With love from your son David." My mother looked at the painting. Then she said, "Your father is the only real artist in the family."

Linda and I had an amicable divorce. Our children are all in the arts. Sophie is a published poet, Sandor is a professional photographer, and Jeremy is a dramaturgist who began his career as an actor playing all the boys in the film, *The Boys from Brazil,* opposite Gregory Peck and my old friend Laurence Olivier.

Anne and I got married. Anne became a therapist but she doesn't do friends or family.

As I grew older, I began to realize my father was not God, but then there was an incident at the end of his life that, once again, shed confusion on the subject. I had to put my father in a nursing home. When he was dying, he motioned for me to lean over his bed. Then, he whispered, "I absolve you of all your sins."

I was invited to sit at the head table for the opening-night party of the Broadway musical, *State Fair,* at the Tavern on the Green in Central Park. David Merrick was seated next to me in a wheelchair, frozen in mind and body, with an attendant helping him eat. I was seated next to the most famous producer in Broadway history and all

I could think of was how he had tricked me into flying to London to get the rights to *Semi-Detached* so he could bid against me.

I asked Merrick if he remembered me. He stared at me with empty eyes. I reminded him of *Semi-Detached* and our lunch at Sardi's when he wished me success with the play. There was no flicker of recognition. Then I reminded Merrick of how I flew to London and offered Oscar Lewenstein $500 for the rights to *Semi-Detached*. I also reminded him of how he bid $600. No response. When I told him the bidding went to $5,000, Merrick was trying to say something. At $10,000, he was struggling. When I told him I bid $25,000, David Merrick smiled.